100

30-SECOND
PHILOSOPHIES

30-SECOND
PHILOSOPHIES

The 50 most thought-provoking
philosophies, each explained
in half a minute

Consultant Editor
Barry Loewer

Foreword
Stephen Law

Contributors
Julian Baggini
Kati Balog
James Garvey
Barry Loewer
Jeremy Stangroom

Published in the UK in 2010 by
Icon Books Ltd
Omnibus Business Centre
39–41 North Road, London N7 9DP
email: info@iconbooks.co.uk
www.iconbooks.co.uk

This book was conceived, designed
and produced by
Ivy Press
210 High Street, Lewes,
East Sussex BN7 2NS, UK
www.ivy-group.co.uk

Creative Director **Peter Bridgewater**
Publisher **Jason Hook**
Editorial Director **Caroline Earle**
Art Director **Michael Whitehead**
Commissioning Editor **Nic Compton**
Designers **James Hollywell, Les Hunt**
Concept Design **Linda Becker**
Illustrations **Ivan Hissey**
Glossaries Text **James Garvey**
Picture Research **Lynda Marshall**

ISBN: 978-1-848311-62-6

Printed and bound in China

10 9 8 7 6 5 4 3 2

CONTENTS

FOREWORD
Stephen Law

Philosophy addresses what are sometimes called the 'big questions'. These include questions about morality ('What makes things morally right or wrong?'); about what we can know, if anything ('Can you know that the world around you is real, and not a computer-generated virtual reality?'); about the nature of human existence ('Are you your brain? Do we possess souls?'); and about the nature of reality ('Why is there anything at all?').

Religion addresses many of the same questions, but while philosophy and religion overlap in the questions they address, they can differ in the approach they take to answering them. While faith and revelation are typically the cornerstones of religious belief, philosophy places great emphasis on reason – on applying our intelligence in order to figure out, as best we can, what the answers are.

Socrates is supposed to have said, 'The unexamined life is not worth living.' That's a strong claim – too strong, I think. Suppose someone devotes themselves selflessly to helping and enriching the lives of their friends, family and wider community. They can hardly be said to have led a worthless existence simply because they never bothered to step back and ask themselves a philosophical question.

Having said that, I've no doubt a little exposure to philosophy can be valuable. The kind of skills philosophy fosters – such as the ability to spot a logical fallacy, or to make a point succinctly and with precision – are the kind of 'transferable' skills that employers value. A little training in philosophy can also help us build robust critical defences and immunize us against the wiles of pretentious wafflers and quacks. But they're not the only reason why a little philosophical reflection can be worthwhile.

Whether we realize it or not, we all hold philosophical beliefs. That God exists is a philosophical belief, as is the belief that he doesn't. That right and wrong are not just a matter of subjective opinion is a philosophical belief, as is the belief that they are. Many of us go through life without even registering that we hold philosophical beliefs, let alone questioning them. You may ask: 'What does it matter whether we ask such questions? After all, the beliefs and the lives of those who ponder them usually aren't much different to the beliefs and lives of those who don't. So why bother?' Perhaps because the unexamined life is not a life chosen freely in awareness of alternatives, but a furrow mindlessly plowed.

If that doesn't convince you that a little philosophy is a good idea – well, there remains the fact that, good for you or not, *philosophy is fun*. Within these pages you'll find some of the most intriguing, clever, astonishing and sometimes downright disturbing ideas ever entertained by mankind. Dip in and find out.

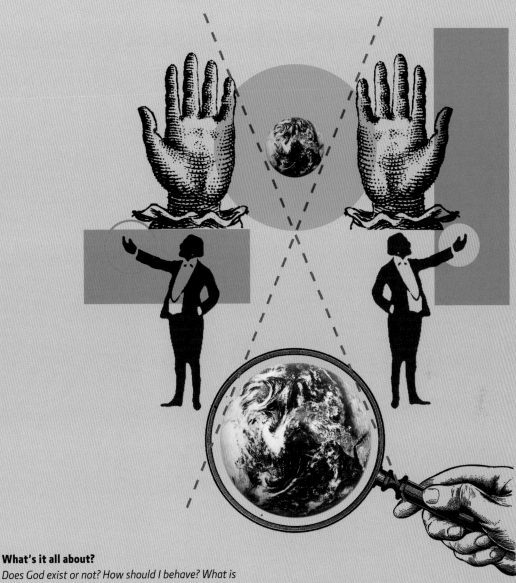

What's it all about?

*Does God exist or not? How should I behave? What is
real? How do we know what we know? In this book,
leading philosophical writers will engage your thought
processes with a crash course in understanding the
foundations of understanding.*

Platonic idealism
The 'big' questions began with the great Greek philosophers. According to Plato, everything in the world is a reflection of its true ideal form that exists outside the world. Plato likened this experience to the flickering shadows of objects reflected on a cave wall by firelight (see page 120).

INTRODUCTION
Barry Loewer

Philosophy tries to get to the bottom of things

by asking questions and proposing answers. At the bottom of science, for example, are questions like, 'What are the aims of the sciences?'; 'What is scientific method and why is it so successful?'; 'What is a scientific law?'; 'What is time?'; and so on. Scientists generally don't stop to consider fundamental questions like these since they are too busy working on science itself. They can get along by accepting, implicitly or implicitly, certain views without questioning them. Thinking about questions at the bottom of things and developing systematic accounts of the foundations of science is left to the philosophers of science.

Other branches of philosophy concern the foundations of ethics, art, religion, mathematics, psychology, language and thought in general. Indeed, for every subject and human enterprise there is a philosophy of that subject that delves into the foundations of the subject. The most general branches of philosophy are ontology (about what there is), epistemology (about how and how much we can know about what there is), and ethics (about what we ought to do about what there is).

Philosophers have been thinking about at-the-bottom questions for at least 2,500 years. It started with the great Greek philosophers Socrates, Plato and Aristotle and has continued to the present day when most (but not all) philosophers are also university professors. Philosophy has evolved as a kind of conversation through the ages among these philosophers. For example, the question 'What is knowledge?' was asked by the Greeks, their answers discussed by medieval philosophers, and their answers much debated and added to by the 17th- and 18th-century philosophers Descartes, Leibniz and Hume. A contemporary philosopher who addresses this question will have one eye on this history and another on what his contemporaries are saying. In the course of this ongoing conversation many problems, positions and paradoxes have been produced. In this book you will find a sampling of these.

HOW TO BECOME A PHILOSOPHER (IN A LITTLE MORE THAN) 30 SECONDS

Barry Loewer

If you are sceptical that you can become a philosopher in 30 seconds, then you have taken a first small step towards becoming one. The attitude of scepticism and the inclination to question are central to philosophy. By questioning your (and others') beliefs with an open mind, you will better understand what it is you believe, what your concepts are, and thus come to know yourself better. Although it is not possible for you to become a philosopher (you may be one already) by just reading this text, I can pose some of the questions that may take you a bit farther along the path.

Most of us take it for granted that we ought to keep promises. But is this always true? What if Burt promises to return Hilary's gun, but learns that Hilary intends to use it to shoot Willard. Should Burt return the gun? Suppose you think, 'No, not in this case.' If so, your next philosophical move may be to look for a general principle that specifies when promises ought to be kept. Perhaps you think the correct rule is: 'Keep a promise, unless keeping it will harm someone.' (This isn't quite right either, since keeping your promise to be faithful to your spouse may harm your lover.)

Next, ask yourself: 'Why ought we to obey this or any proposed rule of ethics?' Some people think that we ought to obey ethical rules because God commanded it. But even if you believe that God exists this isn't correct, since (as Socrates would have said) keeping your promises is not right because God commanded it, but rather God commanded it because it is right. So why is it right? If you explore what philosophers have said about this question over the past 2,500 years, you will discover that there is a lot of disagreement.

Some people conclude that thinking about these questions is a waste of time because agreement will never be reached. But a few people are exhilarated by the process of questioning, thinking about tentative answers, questioning deeper, and so on. Even if we don't settle many of these questions, the process brings us closer to understanding ourselves.

Think about it

If you are already wondering why this book exists, then you are well on your way to becoming a philosopher.

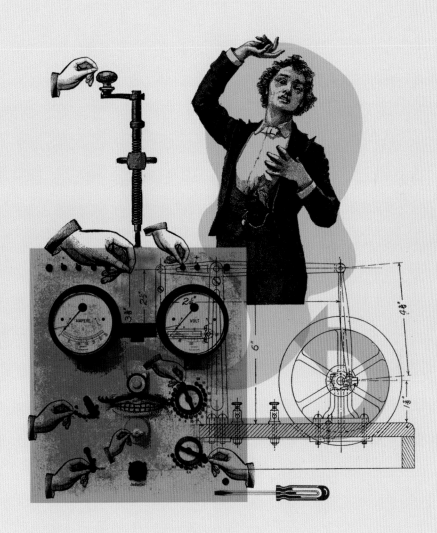

LANGUAGE & LOGIC

LANGUAGE & LOGIC
GLOSSARY

argument A collection of premises offered in support of a conclusion. For example: (1) All men are mortal; (2) Socrates is a man; (3) Therefore, Socrates is mortal.

conclusion The statement that an argument attempts to prove. In the argument '(1) All men are mortal; (2) Socrates is a man; (3) Therefore, Socrates is mortal,' (3) is the conclusion.

deduction An inference from a general claim to a particular conclusion. For example: all snails eat lettuce, this thing is a snail, therefore this thing eats lettuce.

definite description An expression that picks out a person, place or thing, for example, 'The last man standing'.

induction An inference from many particular claims to a general claim, or to other particular claims. For example: this snail eats lettuce, this snail eats lettuce, this one too, etc, therefore, all snails eat lettuce.

inference A mental movement from premises to a conclusion. Sometimes also used as a synonym for 'argument'.

logic The study of inference. Logic itself has many branches and manifestations, from informal logic (which examines the structure of argumentation in natural languages) to formal logic (the study of the purely abstract, formal structure of inference), to the study of such things as mathematical reasoning, modality, computer science, fallacies, probability and much else.

logical form This is revealed through an analysis of the hidden logical structure underlying the superficial syntax of propositions, according to some philosophers. Bertrand Russell, for example, argued that one can get around certain problems associated with referring to something that does not exist by unpacking the hidden logical form of certain suspect expressions.

paradox This involves a certain sort of tension between two claims that seem obviously true. The trouble often comes when conflicting claims seem to follow logically from something else thought to be true.

predicate The part of a proposition that attributes something to the subject. That which is stated or asserted about the subject. For example, in the proposition, 'Socrates is drunk', 'drunk' is the predicate.

premise A statement advanced in support of a conclusion. In the argument '(1) All men are mortal; (2) Socrates is a man; (3) Therefore, Socrates is mortal,' (1) and (2) are premises.

reference The object referred to by an expression, according to some philosophers of language, and logicians. For example, the reference of 'Mark Twain' is the actual person, Mark Twain.

sense The cognitive significance of an expression, or the way in which something is expressed, according to some philosophers of language, and logicians. For example, the expressions 'Mark Twain' and 'Samuel Clemens' refer to just the same thing, exactly one person. The difference between the expressions, then, has to do with their different senses.

subject The part of a proposition about which something is attributed. For example, in the proposition, 'Socrates is drunk', 'Socrates' is the subject.

validity The way premises and conclusions hang together logically in successful arguments. If the premises are true and the argument is valid, then the conclusion has to be true.

ARISTOTLE'S SYLLOGISMS
the 30-second philosophy

3-SECOND THRASH
An inference (or argument)
is valid when it is impossible
for its premises to be true
and its conclusion false.

3-MINUTE THOUGHT
In the 20th century two
great mathematical
results were proved
concerning first order
logic: it is complete, and
it is undecidable. Kurt
Gödel demonstrated
that it is possible to
program a computer
to list all the valid
inferences (completeness),
and Alonzo Church
demonstrated that it is
impossible to program a
computer to determine
whether or not every
inference is valid
(undecidability).

More than 2,300 years ago,
Aristotle noticed that in certain inferences
it is impossible for their premises to be true
and their conclusions false. An example is the
inference from 'All men are mortals' and 'All
mortals fear death' to 'All men fear death'. In
modern logic, such inferences are said to be
deductively valid. Aristotle discovered that the
validity of an inference depends not on its
subject matter, but only on the form of the
premises and conclusion. All inferences of the
form 'All Fs are Gs, and All Gs are Hs, therefore
All Fs are Hs' are valid. He described a number
of such forms, which are called 'syllogisms'.
Until the 19th century, the subject of logic
pretty much consisted of Aristotle's syllogisms.
But syllogisms are only a small portion of all
valid inferences, and do not include many
of the patterns of valid inference that are
employed in science and mathematics. In 1879
Gottlob Frege devised a much more general
characterization of valid inference that is
sufficient for representing mathematical and
scientific reasoning. A descendant of Frege's
system, called 'First Order Logic with Identity',
is now generally thought to be capable of
representing mathematical theories and proofs,
and is taught to all philosophy students.

RELATED PHILOSOPHIES
see also
RUSSELL'S PARADOX &
FREGE'S LOGICISM
page 14

**3-SECOND
BIOGRAPHIES**
ARISTOTLE
384–322 BC

GOTTLOB FREGE
1848–1925

KURT GÖDEL
1906–1978

ALONZO CHURCH
1903–1995

30-SECOND TEXT
Barry Loewer

*To Aristotle it was
logical – we are
people, we are going
to die, and therefore
we are frightened.
Thanks a lot, Aristotle!*

RUSSELL'S PARADOX & FREGE'S LOGICISM

the 30-second philosophy

Bertrand Russell thought up a deep and perplexing paradox when reading about Gottlob Frege's system of logic. Frege thought that he could define all mathematical concepts and prove all mathematical truths solely from principles of logic. The view that mathematics can be reduced to logic in this way is called logicism. Had Frege demonstrated the truth of logicism, it would have been one of the greatest achievements in the history of philosophy. But his version of logicism was not successful. One of the logical principles used to prove the existence of numbers, functions and other mathematical objects is: for every predicate, 'is F (P)' there is a collection of things that are F. Two examples are: 'is a prime number' determines the collection of numbers {2, 3, 5, 7, 1....} and 'is a collection' determines the collection of all collections. In 1903 Russell showed that (P) is self-contradictory with the following argument. Consider the predicate 'is not a member of itself'. With (P) there is a collection—call it R—of collections that are not members of themselves. Is R a member of itself? If it is then it isn't, and if it isn't then it is. A contradiction! This was a devastating blow to Frege and to logicism.

He who shaves the shavers, shaves the least or the most? Either way, did anyone think about growing a beard?

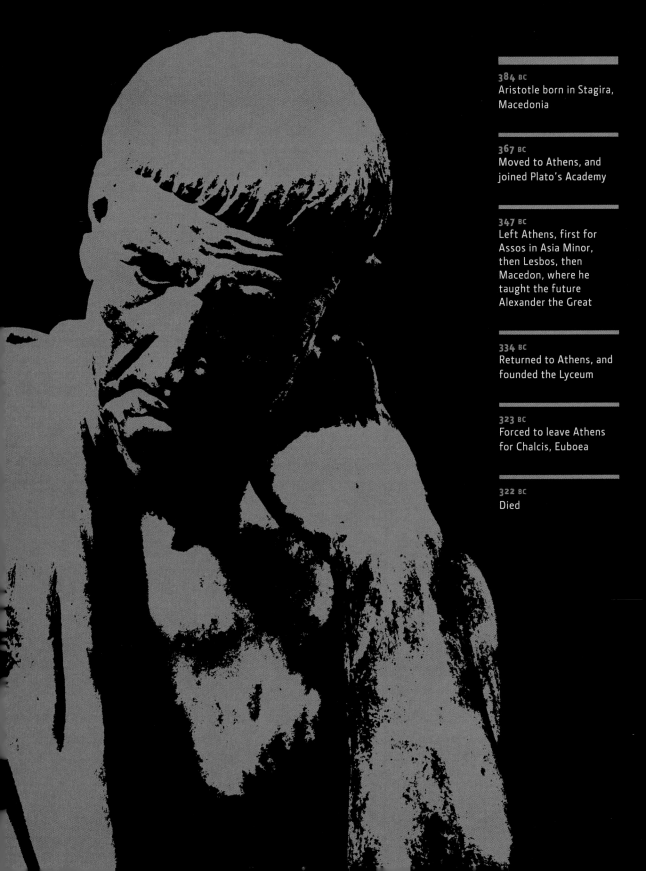

384 BC
Aristotle born in Stagira,
Macedonia

367 BC
Moved to Athens, and
joined Plato's Academy

347 BC
Left Athens, first for
Assos in Asia Minor,
then Lesbos, then
Macedon, where he
taught the future
Alexander the Great

334 BC
Returned to Athens, and
founded the Lyceum

323 BC
Forced to leave Athens
for Chalcis, Euboea

322 BC
Died

ARISTOTLE

It would be hard to exaggerate the importance of Aristotle to the history of philosophy. As well as formalizing the rules of deduction, he undertook groundbreaking work in the fields of ethics, politics, metaphysics, biology, physics, psychology, aesthetics, poetry, rhetoric, cosmology, mathematics and the philosophy of mind.

Aristotle was born in 384 BC, in the Macedonian city of Stagira, now in northern Greece. He was the son of Nicomachus, a physician to the court of the king of Macedon, who sent him to Athens in 367 BC, where he joined Plato's Academy, remaining there for 20 years, first as a student and later as a teacher. After Plato's death, Aristotle left Athens, eventually ending up in Macedon, where he tutored the future Alexander the Great. He then returned to Athens, and founded his own school, the Lyceum or Peripatetic school (likely so called because he taught while strolling along the covered walkways of the Lyceum). Aristotle remained in Athens until he ran into trouble in 323 BC as anti-Macedonian sentiment swept the city, and charges of 'impiety' were laid against him. Insisting that he would not allow the Athenians to 'sin twice against philosophy', he left Athens for the city of Chalcis, where he died the following year of a digestive illness.

Unfortunately, we know less about the circumstances in which Aristotle produced his great works than we do about his life. It is likely that most of his surviving treatises were not intended for publication, but rather were assembled and edited from lecture notes by his successors. This in part explains why they are hard to read – full of technical language, detailed discussion, inconsistencies and *lacunae*. His work, nevertheless, remains one of the crowning achievements of the classical world, and probably unparalleled in its importance for the development of the discipline of philosophy.

RUSSELL'S THEORY OF DESCRIPTIONS

the 30-second philosophy

Bertrand Russell claimed that the reference of an expression is its meaning. At first he thought that the meaning of a definite description, for example 'the present king of France', was some particular object, in this case a particular king. But at that time France had no king, so Russell thought that the king must exist in some way, even though he couldn't be found in our world. Soon enough, Russell came to think that this was too much ontology to swallow and proposed his theory of descriptions to avoid this consequence, while holding onto the idea that reference is meaning. His idea is that 'the present king of France' doesn't have a meaning on its own, but any sentence in which this phrase occurs can be translated into a sentence in which the phrase doesn't occur. 'The present king of France is bald' is translated into 'There is one and only one present king of France, and he is bald'. If this is correct, then the original sentence with the definite description is false. Russell said that the second sentence revealed the logical form of the first sentence. Since the phrase 'the present king of France' doesn't occur in this sentence there is no need for a particular king to exist for the sentence to have meaning.

3-SECOND THRASH
The logical form of the statement: 'The present king of France is bald' is given by 'There is one and only one king of France, and he is bald'.

3-MINUTE THOUGHT
Underlying Russell's theory is the idea that a sentence has a 'logical form' that makes its meaning and its logic easily understood. This idea was very influential on subsequent philosophers and linguists, including Ludwig Wittgenstein and Noam Chomsky.

RELATED PHILOSOPHIES
see also
FREGE'S PUZZLE
page 24
WITTGENSTEIN'S PICTURE THEORY OF LANGUAGE
page 138

3-SECOND BIOGRAPHIES
BERTRAND RUSSELL
1872–1970

LUDWIG WITTGENSTEIN
1889–1951

NOAM CHOMSKY
1928–

30-SECOND TEXT
Barry Loewer

Whatever Bertrand Russell says, this is definitely not the present king of France. He just wears the crown to cover his bald patch.

FREGE'S PUZZLE
the 30-second philosophy

3-SECOND THRASH
If 'Hesperus' and 'Phosphorus' are just different names for the same thing – the planet Venus – how can it be that 'Hesperus is Phosphorus' and 'Hesperus is Hesperus' differ in meaning?

3-MINUTE THOUGHT
Many philosophers find the notion of sense obscure. The logician Saul Kripke argued that proper names do not have senses at all. In his view the reference of a proper name is not determined by a sense but by a chain of uses of the name that begins with an act of naming. For example, you may use the name 'Thales' to refer to a certain pre-Socratic philosopher even though you don't know anything about him, as long as you acquired the name from someone who used it to refer to Thales.

In his early writings on language, the great logician Gottlob Frege held that the meaning of a name is its reference. For example, the meaning of the name 'Mont Blanc' is the mountain itself. But, in later writings, Frege argued that two names may have the same reference, yet differ in meaning. He reasoned that if the meaning of a name is just its reference, and two names have the same reference, then it should make no difference to the meaning of a sentence which name occurs in it. Since 'Hesperus' and 'Phosphorus' are both names of the planet Venus, (1) 'Hesperus is Phosphorus' and (2) 'Hesperus is Hesperus' should have the same meaning. But Frege observed that they do differ in meaning, since (1) expresses a significant astronomical discovery, while (2) is a triviality. The explanation of why they differ in meaning is Frege's Puzzle. Frege's solution is that the meaning of a name is not only its reference, but also its sense. The sense of a name is a condition that picks out the individual (if there is one) that satisfies that condition as the name's reference. Frege says that 'Hesperus' and 'Phosphorus' have different senses that pick out the same reference. This, he says, explains how (1) can be informative, while (2) is a triviality. Much 20th-century philosophy of language involves a discussion of Frege's notion of sense.

RELATED PHILOSOPHIES
see also
RUSSELL'S PARADOX & FREGE'S LOGICISM
page 18

RUSSELL'S THEORY OF DESCRIPTIONS
page 22

3-SECOND BIOGRAPHY
GOTTLOB FREGE
1848–1925

30-SECOND TEXT
Barry Loewer

You say Phosphorus, I say Hersperus. Let's call the whole thing off – and just call it Venus.

GÖDEL'S THEOREM

the 30-second philosophy

RELATED PHILOSOPHIES
see also
EPIMENIDES' LIAR PARADOX
page 28

3-SECOND BIOGRAPHIES
KURT GÖDEL
1906–1978

ROGER PENROSE
1931–

30-SECOND TEXT
Barry Loewer

3-SECOND THRASH
For any (sufficiently strong) mathematical theory, there are true statements that cannot be proved in that theory.

3-MINUTE THOUGHT
Some philosophers, and the physicist Roger Penrose, have claimed that Gödel's theorem shows that our minds do not work like computers. Following a program is analogous to proving a theorem. Gödel showed that, for any axiom system, the statement that the system is consistent cannot be proved by the system itself. So, if our minds operated like a computer following a program, we could not recognize that we are consistent. But we seem able to recognize our own consistency, therefore our minds do not work like computers.

Gödel's theorem is the most profound result in mathematical logic. It is thought to have important philosophical consequences for the limits of knowledge and the nature of mind. In the system of modern logic, it is possible to express arithmetical statements, for example, 'For any pair of numbers n and m, n + m = m + n'. It is also possible to write down axioms (called 'Peano's axioms'), from which one can prove many mathematical truths. The question arose of whether one can prove from these axioms all arithmetical truths, without proving any false statements. Kurt Gödel answered this question negatively. First, he discovered a coding whereby arithmetical statements also have an interpretation in which they are about themselves and what can be proved from various axioms. He then found an arithmetical statement (K) that says under the coding '(K) is not provable'. He reasoned that if (K) is provable then the axioms prove a false statement. But if (K) is not provable then it is true, and there is a truth that the axioms don't prove. Not only are there arithmetical truths that cannot be proved from Peano's axioms, but also any true axioms will leave out some truths as unprovable. This is known as 'Gödel's incompleteness theorem'. It seems to establish a limit on what mathematicians can know.

Even by replacing his brain with a computer, Kurt was unable to figure out those unknowable truths.

EPIMENIDES' LIAR PARADOX

the 30-second philosophy

Epimenides was a sixth-century

BC Cretan philosopher who is reputed to have said, 'All Cretans are liars'. If his utterance is true then he is lying, and what he said is false. This is an ancient version of what has come to be known as 'the liar paradox'. A contemporary version is based on '1. Sentence 1 is not true.' If sentence 1 is true then it is not true, and if it is not true then it is true. The paradox arises because it seems to be part of the meaning of 'is true' that, where S can be any sentence, one can validly infer 'S' is true from S and also validly infer S from 'S' is true. From 1 we can infer both that S is true and that S is not true. A paradox! The most famous response to the liar paradox came from the logician Alfred Tarski, who distinguished a language (L) from a meta-language (ML), in which one can refer to sentences of L. It is possible to define 'is true in L' in ML without paradox.

RELATED PHILOSOPHIES
see also
GÖDEL'S THEOREM
page 26

3-SECOND THRASH
This sentence is false.

3-MINUTE THOUGHT
The concept of truth is too important to philosophy and scientific thinking to overlook, so there have been many attempts to solve the liar paradox. Tarski's idea gives up on there being a single concept of truth applicable to all languages. Other philosophers have responded by restricting inferences from S to 'S' is true, and some have even developed logics in which certain contradictions are acceptable.

3-SECOND BIOGRAPHIES
EPIMENIDES
Sixth century BC

ALFRED TARSKI
1901–1983

30-SECOND TEXT
Barry Loewer

Which one of you said, 'The truth is rarely pure and never simple'? Whoever it was, you're a liar.

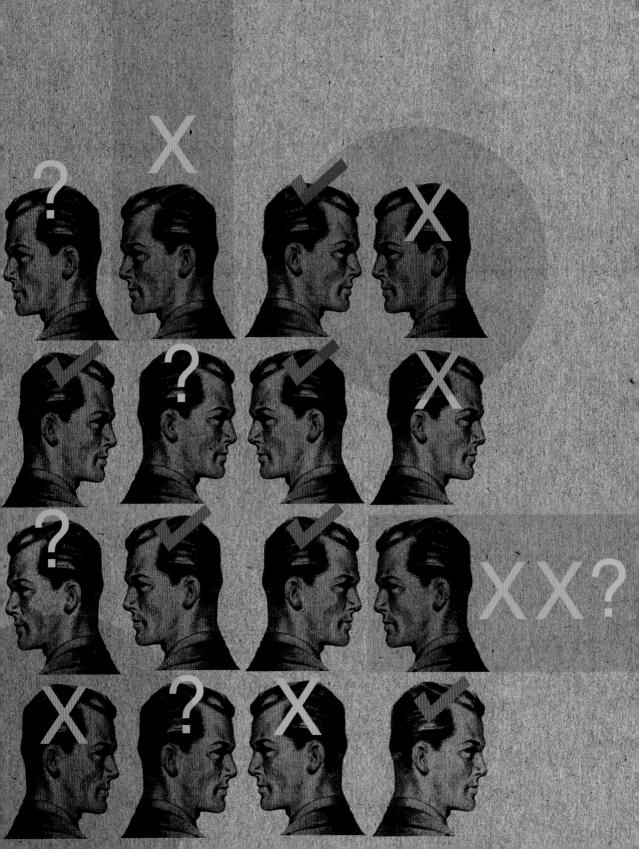

EUBULIDES' HEAP

the 30-second philosophy

Weighing in at 100 kilos

(220.462 pounds), Harry is a fat man. He won't stop being fat if his weight drops to 99.999 kilos (220.460 pounds). So that means any man who weighs the same as Harry must also be fat: a fraction of a gram, or an ounce, can never make the difference between being fat or thin. But, if that's true, then someone who weighs 99.998 kilos (220.457 pounds) is also fat, and so is someone who weighs 99.997 kilos (220.455 pounds), and so on. You'll still be claiming that a fraction of a gram, or an ounce, can't make the difference between fat and thin when you're comparing the person who weighs 40 kilos (88.184 pounds) to one who weighs 39.999 kilos (88.182 pounds). But this is absurd: someone who weights 40 kilos (88.184 pounds) could never be described as fat. Hence the paradox: a series of apparently logically watertight steps leads us to a conclusion that is manifestly false. But neither the logic nor the observation have any evident flaws. This is a version of Eubulides paradox of the heap, where a similar argument showed that a heap would still be a heap when it contained only one grain of sand, just as long as the grains were removed one by one.

3-SECOND BIOGRAPHY
EUBULIDES
Fourth century BC

30-SECOND TEXT
Julian Baggini

3-SECOND THRASH
Why you can never make a mountain out of a molehill.

3-MINUTE THOUGHT
What might this paradox show? That concepts such as fat and thin are vague, so it is a mistake to ever treat them as though there were factual questions to which they definitely apply? Or is it that, counter-intuitively, there is a firm boundary between fat and thin, a heap and a small pile, and that, if you step across it by one grain or 1 gram, the correct description changes?

The journey from being a thin man to being a fat man and back again begins with a single gram.

SCIENCE & EPISTEMOLOGY

SCIENCE & EPISTEMOLOGY
GLOSSARY

circular argument Consists of premises offered in support of a conclusion, where the conclusion is not just one of the premises. Here is a famous example: everything I clearly and distinctly perceive is true, I know this because God created me and He is no deceiver, and I know that because I clearly and distinctly perceive it, and everything I clearly and distinctly perceive is true.

deduction An inference from a general claim to a particular conclusion. For example: all snails eat lettuce, this thing is a snail, therefore this thing eats lettuce.

dualism A metaphysical viewpoint that holds that, ultimately, the Universe is made of just two types of stuff: physical stuff and mental stuff.

epistemology A branch of philosophy that is concerned with the study of human knowledge – its nature, its sources and its limitations.

external world The world of objects as they exist apart from our experience of them, as opposed to our inner worlds of thoughts, perceptions, feelings and the like.

Gettier cases Counter examples to the traditional view of knowledge as justified, true belief. A story is told in which someone has a justified, true belief which, perhaps because of luck, does not count as knowledge. They are named in honour of the person who first formulated them, Edmund Gettier.

induction An inference from many particular claims to a general claim, or to other particular claims. For example: this snail eats lettuce, this snail eats lettuce, this one too, etc, therefore, all snails eat lettuce. There is a problem with induction, however, made famous by David Hume, and a new riddle of induction, created by Nelson Goodman.

inductive rule A principle that legitimizes an inference from many particular claims to a general conclusion, usually thought to be the basis of inductive inferences. There are several candidates: the Universe is uniform, the future will be like the past, everything everywhere is regular, etc.

inference A mental movement from premises to a conclusion. Sometimes also used as a synonym for 'argument'.

justification Evidence or reasons that are presented in support of the truth of a belief or statement.

paradigm A collection of beliefs and agreements shared by scientists (partly implicitly), which guides their research, identifies problems, and tells them what counts as a solution, a good experiment, and much else.

relativism A collection of views that claim that one sort of thing (e.g. morality) depends on something else (e.g. cultural values), which varies. Since there's no set of standards that stand out (all cultural values are on a par), there's nothing to choose between various accounts of one sort of thing (hence, morality is relative).

scepticism The view that knowledge in some domains is not possible, perhaps because justifying our claims to knowledge claims is not possible. Scepticism can be local and directed at some of our alleged knowledge (e.g. scepticism about miraculous claims), or radical and directed at all of our alleged knowledge.

thought experiment An imagined case designed to put pressure on our intuitions, and perhaps clarify the way we think of something. For philosophers, thought experiments are like test tubes that separate a part of the mental world from everything else so that we can have a clear look at it.

truth According to the oldest conception of truth – made famous by Aristotle – to say of what is that it is, and to say of what is not that it is not, is to speak truly.

I THINK, THEREFORE I AM

the 30-second philosophy

RELATED PHILOSOPHIES
see also
THE BRAIN IN A VAT
page 42

3-SECOND BIOGRAPHY
RENÉ DESCARTES
1596–1650

30-SECOND TEXT
Jeremy Stangroom

3-SECOND THRASH
You can doubt that there are other minds, that humans have bodies, even that philosophers are smart – but you can never doubt there is an 'I' doing the doubting.

3-MINUTE THOUGHT
The trouble with Descartes' method of doubt is that the one indubitable truth, 'I exist', is not sufficient to retrieve knowledge of the world and mathematics. Descartes relied on God for this trick: he first proves that God exists and is not a deceiver. If God is no deceiver, then we are not systematically misled about those things we clearly and distinctly perceive, and which survive rational scrutiny. From here, it is fairly easy to retrieve certain of our beliefs about the world.

René Descartes, perhaps the first great modern philosopher, discovered that much of what he was taught by his Jesuit teachers was doubtful. So troubled by the fact that 'there was no such learning in the world as I had been led to hope', he set out to find the foundations upon which genuine, indubitable knowledge could be built. In *Meditations on First Philosophy*, he employed a technique of radical doubt, with the aim of identifying at least one belief he wouldn't be able to doubt. His method was to examine each one of his beliefs, and then to abandon any of them that it was possible to doubt. In this way, he showed that it is easy enough to doubt the truth of all of our sensory experiences – we might be dreaming, and yet not be aware of it; and, most disconcertingly, that it is possible that we have been deceived about absolutely everything, even the simplest truths of mathematics, by an evil demon. Happily, this technique also establishes that in the very act of doubting we show there must be an 'I' which is doing the doubting. As Descartes put it, 'Cogito ergo sum' ('I am thinking, therefore, I exist').

René was sure he existed – but he wasn't sure about those other two.

GETTIER'S COUNTER-EXAMPLE

the 30-second philosophy

3-SECOND THRASH
Why you can justifiably believe the right thing but not truly know it.

3-MINUTE THOUGHT
Later philosophers responded to Gettier by arguing that the things one has beliefs about and the belief itself must be connected in the right way in order for the belief to count as knowledge. But it's been hard to specify what this right way is. Must the link be reliable, rock-solid or perhaps causal? Some philosophers think we should give up the idea that there are precise criteria for concepts such as knowledge.

What is knowledge? Since Plato, many philosophers have thought it is a kind of justified, true belief. This so-called 'tripartite account' says knowledge has three conditions: (1) to know something you must believe it, (2) it must be true, and (3) your belief that it is true must be justified. Then Edmund Gettier came along. Suppose, he argued, that Smith applies for a job and has a justified belief that Jones will get it. Smith is also justified in believing that Jones has ten coins in his pocket. Smith then applies basic logic and concludes, justifiably, that the person who gets the job will have ten coins in his pocket. In fact, Smith gets the job, and although he didn't realize it, he also had ten coins in his pocket. That means that Smith did indeed have a justified true belief that the person who got the job would have ten coins in his pocket. But surely he didn't know this. He didn't know he had ten coins in his pocket, and didn't even believe he would get the job. He had a justified true belief, but that was luck, not knowledge. There are numerous other such counter-examples to the tripartite account, known as 'Gettier cases'.

3-SECOND BIOGRAPHY
EDMUND GETTIER
1927–

30-SECOND TEXT
Julian Baggini

The only thing Smith really knew was that it was lucky that he got the job – he didn't have much money left.

1 2 3 4 5 6 7 8 9 10

1902
Born, Vienna, Austria-Hungary

1935
Logik der Forschung published

1937
Fled Austria for New Zealand, and took up a post at Canterbury University College

1945
The Open Society and Its Enemies published

1949
Became Professor of Logic and Scientific Method at the London School of Economics

1957
The Poverty of Historicism published

1959
Logik der Forschung finally appears in English as *The Logic of Scientific Discovery* translation

1969
Retires from full-time teaching

1994
Dies in London

KARL POPPER

Although Karl Popper is perhaps best remembered for his 'falsificationism', an idea that shaped the philosophy of science in the second half of the 20th century, the scope of his interests was wide. He produced important work in areas ranging from political philosophy to the philosophy of mind. By the end of his life, his collected papers were voluminous enough to fill 450 cartons at the Popper Archive in the Hoover Institution at Stanford University, California.

Popper was born in Vienna in 1902, the youngest child of middle-class parents of Jewish descent. He was brought up a Lutheran, and educated at the University of Vienna, where he studied philosophy, mathematics, psychology and physics. Although he was attracted to Marxism in his youth and joined the Association of Socialist School Students, he quickly grew tired of the strictures of historical materialism and instead adopted the social liberalism that marked his life.

His first major work, *The Logic of Scientific Discovery*, was published in 1935 (although it wasn't translated into English until 1959).

It was in this book that he outlined his ideas about falsification that so influenced supporters and critics alike. In a remarkable ten-year period, he followed this with *The Poverty of Historicism*, a critique of the idea that history is governed by the operation of laws, and *The Open Society and its Enemies*, a two-volume defence of the principles of social liberalism in the face of the threat from authoritarianism and totalitarianism.

Undoubtedly Karl Popper's political ideas were influenced by personal experience. In 1937, fearful of the rise of Nazism, he left Austria, where he had been working as a schoolteacher, and took up a post as a lecturer in philosophy at Canterbury University College in New Zealand. After the end of World War Two, he joined the faculty at the London School of Economics, becoming Professor of Logic and Scientific Method in 1949, where he remained until his retirement from full-time teaching in 1969. Karl Popper died in 1994, with his reputation assured as one of the most important philosophers of the 20th century.

THE BRAIN IN A VAT

the 30-second philosophy

The 'brain in a vat' thought experiment, a version of which is the premise for *The Matrix* films, tends to be employed to tell us something about our knowledge of the world. It asks us to imagine that a brain has been detached from a person's body, placed into a vat of fluid, and then connected to a device that entirely replicates the electrical impulses that normally come in from the outside world. The idea is that this will produce an experience of a virtual reality that is indistinguishable from the real world. This introduces the problem of radical scepticism. Specifically, it seems possible that we are living in a virtual world, but do not know it. This, in turn, would mean that all our beliefs about the world – for example, that I am currently typing this text on a word processor – are false. If we accept that this is possible, then seemingly we must concede that we cannot know that what we take to be true about the world is, in fact, true. In other words, if it is possible that something like the scenario portrayed in *The Matrix* is true, then we have to accept that there is no secure foundation for our knowledge of the world.

3-SECOND THRASH
You think you're holding this book, reading this sentence, but actually you're a brain in a vat, being fed electrical impulses by a supercomputer located in Boston.

3-MINUTE THOUGHT
The philosopher Hilary Putnam rejects the sceptical implications of the brain in a vat thought experiment. He argues, roughly speaking, that the words that a person uses inside a virtual world refer to the constituent elements of that world, not to the things in a purported outside world. Therefore, whether I am sitting under a tree, for example, depends upon the state of affairs that exists in the particular world that I inhabit (virtual, or otherwise).

RELATED PHILOSOPHIES
see also
I THINK, THEREFORE I AM
page 36

3-SECOND BIOGRAPHY
HILARY PUTNAM
1926–

30-SECOND TEXT
Jeremy Stangroom

Surely you are more than a brain in a vat? Are you certain? Perhaps this is a picture of you.

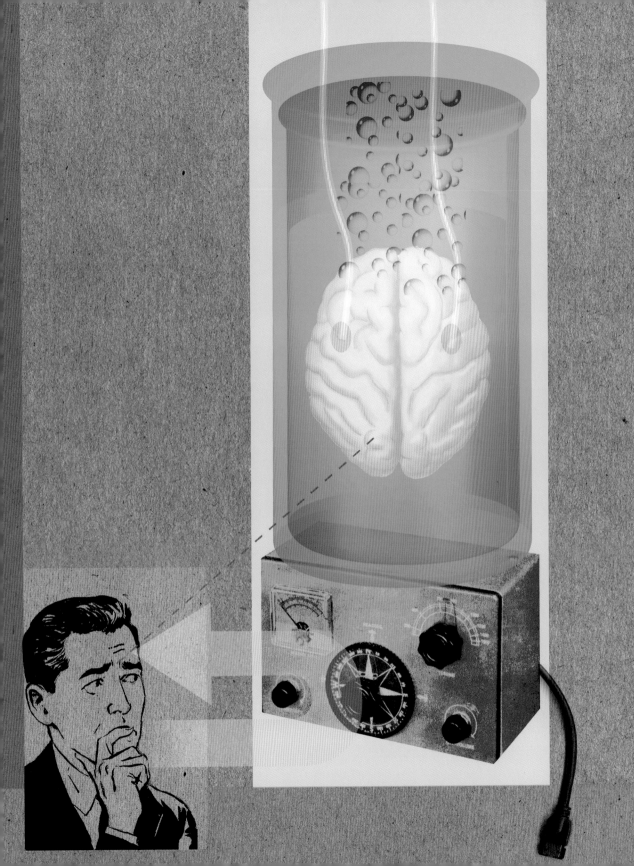

HUME'S PROBLEM OF INDUCTION

the 30-second philosophy

David Hume reflected on the fact that we often reason from what has been observed in the past to what will be observed in the future. For example, from the fact that all emeralds so far observed are green, we may infer that emeralds observed in the future will also be green. This reasoning is called 'an inductive inference'. Hume formulated this rule of induction: infer that regularities observed to hold in the past will be continued into the future. He then observed that inductive inferences following this rule are not deductively valid. It is logically possible for 'all observed emeralds are green' to be true although 'all emeralds are green' is false. Hume asked: 'If inductive inferences are not valid, then why should we think that they reliably lead us towards truths?' Perhaps all the emeralds observed so far are green, but starting tomorrow they will be blue. Hume argued that there cannot be a non-circular argument that shows his inductive rule does lead to truths, even if it generally does. Hume thought that although there is no justification of induction, it is part of our human nature to make inductive inferences. Many philosophers have taken his argument as a challenge to produce a non-circular demonstration that induction is reliable, but so far no one has succeeded and if Hume is right no one ever will.

RELATED PHILOSOPHIES
see also
GOODMAN'S GRUESOME RIDDLE
page 46

POPPER'S CONJECTURES & REFUTATIONS
page 48

3-SECOND BIOGRAPHIES
DAVID HUME
1711–1776

HANS REICHENBACH
1891–1953

MAX BLACK
1909–1988

PETER STRAWSON
1919–2006

30-SECOND TEXT
Barry Loewer

3-SECOND THRASH
How do we know that the future will be like the past?

3-MINUTE THOUGHT
Peter Strawson claimed that the rule of induction requires no justification since part of what it means to be rational is to reason inductively. Max Black claimed that a particular inductive inference can be justified by the rule 'infer that the future will be like the past', and that this rule is justified since it has worked in the past. Hans Reichenbach tried to prove that if there is a reliable way to infer the future from the past, then induction will be reliable. None of these responses meet Hume's challenge head on, since they don't show that the rule of induction is reliable.

As soon as he found the blue emerald, he began to question everything: The Sun had risen every morning of his life so far – but will it come up tomorrow?

GOODMAN'S GRUESOME RIDDLE

the 30-second philosophy

RELATED PHILOSOPHIES
see also
HUME'S PROBLEM OF
INDUCTION
page 44

POPPER'S CONJECTURES
& REFUTATIONS
page 48

3-SECOND BIOGRAPHY
NELSON GOODMAN
1906–1998

30-SECOND TEXT
Barry Loewer

Nelson Goodman claimed that the inductive rule 'infer that past regularities will be continued in the future' cannot be right, since it leads to conflicting conclusions. To illustrate this he defined a predicate 'is grue' as follows: something is grue at time t if, and only if, it is green and t is before the first moment, of the year 2100, or it is blue and t is that moment or later. Suppose all emeralds so far observed are green. Then they are also grue, because they are green and have been observed before 2100. So, the rule of induction tells us to infer that emeralds after the year 2100 will be green, and also that they will be grue. But after the year 2100, grue emeralds are blue not green! Goodman concluded that the rule of induction must be modified to say that the future will be like the past, but only in certain respects that are 'projectible'. The problem is specifying which predicates are projectible, and which aren't. One idea is that 'grue' is not 'projectible' since it is defined in terms of 'green' and 'blue'. But 'green' and 'blue' are just as easily definable in terms of 'grue' and 'bleen'.

3-SECOND THRASH
The rule 'infer that past regularities will be continued in the future' must be modified to apply only to projectible predicates.

3-MINUTE THOUGHT
Prior to Goodman propounding his riddle, Bertrand Russell had already remarked that reasoning that the future will be like the past can lead one astray. He imagined a chicken who observed the farmer having always in the past selected a chicken other than herself for his dinner. Thus the chicken concluded that in the future the farmer would always select a chicken other than herself for his dinner.

On the 25th of the month, the rooster realized that the induction had been wrong all along. He turned grue with fright.

POPPER'S CONJECTURES & REFUTATIONS

the 30-second philosophy

Karl Popper rejected the view that science proceeds by the inductive inference of regularities from observations. To the contrary, he claimed that scientific knowledge grows by a process he called 'conjecture and refutation'. His mantra is: 'You can't prove a hypothesis true, or even have evidence that it is true by induction, but you can refute it if it is false'. Popper held that a good scientific hypothesis is one from which many surprising predictions deductively follow. His crucial point is that if an observation deductively follows from a theory, and if our experiments do not result in the predicted observation, then it follows that the theory itself is false. Popper's view is that scientists should put forward such hypotheses and try their hardest to refute them. If a prediction fails, we learn that the hypothesis is false. This process, he thinks, describes the growth of scientific knowledge from Aristotelian physics, to Newtonian physics, to Einstein's theories of relativity. Popper adds that what makes the claims of astrology, Freudian theory, and Marxism pseudo-scientific is that their practitioners don't even try to refute them, and argue away apparent refutations.

RELATED PHILOSOPHIES
see also
HUME'S PROBLEM OF INDUCTION
page 44

GOODMAN'S GRUESOME RIDDLE
page 46

KUHN'S SCIENTIFIC REVOLUTIONS
page 50

3-SECOND BIOGRAPHIES
KARL POPPER
1902–1994

GEORGE SOROS
1930–

30-SECOND TEXT
Barry Loewer

3-SECOND THRASH
Science grows by a process of conjecture and refutation.

3-MINUTE THOUGHT
The financier and philanthropist George Soros was Popper's student at the London School of Economics. He made billions of dollars with his investments and currency trading. Soros says that he used Popper's method of conjecture and refutation to help decide on investments, and credits it with his success.

Karl's brain grew so large that he realized that the only thing that he knew to be true was that he would never know what was true, only what was false.

$E=mc^2$

KUHN'S SCIENTIFIC REVOLUTIONS

the 30-second philosophy

RELATED PHILOSOPHIES
see also
POPPER'S CONJECTURES &
REFUTATIONS
page 48

3-SECOND BIOGRAPHY
THOMAS KUHN
1922–1996

30-SECOND TEXT
Jeremy Stangroom

3-SECOND THRASH
The work of scientific communities is driven by the demands of particular scientific paradigms, which rule the roost until better paradigms come along.

3-MINUTE THOUGHT
The major problem of Thomas Kuhn's approach is that it suggests a certain kind of relativism about truth. If the rules and criteria for assessing truth claims only work within paradigms, then it isn't possible to adjudicate between their competing claims. There is also no way to determine the overall merits of particular paradigms, since there is no view from the outside upon which to base such an assessment.

In his classic work, *The Structure of Scientific Revolutions*, Thomas Kuhn argues that what he calls 'normal science' takes place within the context of particular paradigms, which provide the rules and standards for scientific practice within any particular scientific discipline. Paradigms allow scientists to develop avenues of inquiry, to create fruitful research strategies, to construct questions, to interpret results and to analyze their relevance and meaning. It is Kuhn's claim that the history of science is marked by periodic 'scientific revolutions', each of which sees the dominant paradigm in a particular field replaced by a new paradigm (as, for example, occurred when the Ptolemaic worldview was overthrown by the Copernican system). A scientific revolution is preceded by a period of crisis, during which it becomes clear that, under pressure from a growing number of puzzles and difficulties, an existing paradigm can no longer be maintained. A revolution occurs when the scientific community moves its allegiance to a new paradigm, signalling the end of the crisis, and the resumption of normal science. Kuhn does not accept this pattern of continually changing paradigms means that science does not progress. He argues that modern scientific theories are better than earlier ones at solving puzzles that arise in many different conditions.

After a scientific revolution, or 'paradigm shift', many scientific theories turn out to be garbage.

MIND & METAPHYSICS

MIND & METAPHYSICS
GLOSSARY

aboutness A distinctive characteristic of thoughts, desires, words, pictures and the like, also called 'intentionality'. Such things seem to point beyond themselves. A word is directed towards or about something other than the ink on the page. A rock isn't about anything.

behaviourism A family of views that reduces talk of mental things (such as dreams, hopes and beliefs), or even the mental things themselves to behaviour, i.e. the observable activities or movements of bodies.

conceivability A state of affairs is conceivable if you can think of it without contradiction. Importantly, conceivability is thought to be a guide to possibility – whatever is conceivable is possible. Maybe there's no contradiction in thinking of kangaroos without tails, so such things are possible, but a four-sided triangle is inconceivable and, therefore, not possible. Similar thoughts might have large implications for the philosophy of mind.

consciousness The aspect of our mental lives variously described as wakefulness, awareness, or our experience of the world. Thomas Nagel famously argues that there is something it is like to be a conscious creature, something it is like for that creature. The 'something it is like' is consciousness.

determinism The view that every event, without exception, is fully caused by its antecedent conditions, i.e. the events leading up to it. Rewind the Universe back to 2001 and run it forwards again and everything will happen exactly as it did before. What seem like free choices and actions are thought to be determined, too.

dualism A metaphysical view which holds that, ultimately, the Universe is made of just two types of stuff: physical stuff and mental stuff.

epiphenomenalism A view of the mind-body relation that holds that all, or almost all, mental phenomena are merely the by-products (epiphenomena) of physical interactions. In this view, mental events might cause other mental events, but mental phenomena have no physical effects.

free will The organ of origination, the part of us that allegedly makes free choices, somehow not bound by causal laws. Those who hold that the will is free claim, contrary to determinists, that we sometimes have the power to twist ourselves free of the causal web, and just choose what course of action to take.

metaphysics The branch of philosophy that is concerned with the nature of reality.

monism The view that, ultimately, reality is made up of just one kind of thing.

natural languages Languages like English and German, as opposed to 'artificial languages' such as computer-programming languages and, if Jerry Fodor is right, something else – the language of thought, which is prior to all other languages.

paradox In general, paradoxes involve a certain sort of conflict or tension between two claims that seem obviously true. The trouble often comes when conflicting claims seem to follow logically from something thought to be true.

personal identity Whatever it is that makes you the same you over time. The main candidates are the continuity of your body over time, and the continuity of your mind over time.

raw feels The peculiar way some mental states strike us: e.g. the pangs of hunger, the sting of jealousy, the sharpness of the taste of a green apple, the hurtfulness of pain and the goofy twinge of a tickle.

DESCARTES' MIND-BODY PROBLEM

the 30-second philosophy

3-SECOND THRASH
Is your mind a non-physical, ghostly kind of thing that controls your body, is it your brain or is it something else entirely?

3-MINUTE THOUGHT
Descartes thought that the laws of physics leave room for minds to affect the motions of the pineal gland (and the body). But as physics has advanced, many philosophers have become convinced that all the motions of physical bodies are governed by the laws of physics. This makes it especially difficult to understand how the mind can affect the body, unless it is itself physical.

In his *Meditations*, René Descartes formulated the mind-body problem. The problem is understanding how consciousness, minds, thoughts and free choice are related to the material world described by science. Descartes argued that mind and body are distinct substances, with very different essential features. Mind, he said, is essentially thinking, non-spatial, and can initiate free choice. Body is essentially extended in space, non-thinking, and governed by the laws of motion. Descartes' own view, dualist interactionism, is that in a living person mind and body are united, and each is constantly influencing the other. But how can mind affect body if the latter is governed by the laws of nature? Descartes' answer was that mind and body interact in a human being at a point inside the pineal gland (a small gland located at the base of the brain). This answer didn't satisfy subsequent philosophers, who have come up with many alternative theories. Among these are: physicalism, the view that mind and body are not really distinct, and mind is really physical; idealism, which holds that body is really an illusion, and only mind exists; monism, which says that reality has both mental and physical aspects; and epiphenomenalism, the view that body can affect mind, but mind cannot affect body.

RELATED PHILOSOPHIES
see also
BRENTANO'S INTENTIONALITY
page 58

LAPLACE'S DEMON, DETERMINISM, & FREE WILL
page 74

RYLE'S GHOST IN THE MACHINE
page 76

3-SECOND BIOGRAPHIES
RENÉ DESCARTES
1596–1650

ARTHUR SCHOPENHAUER
1788–1860

30-SECOND TEXT
Kati Balog

The philosopher Arthur Schopenhauer called the mind-body problem, 'The World Knot'. It has yet to be untied.

BRENTANO'S INTENTIONALITY

the 30-second philosophy

3-SECOND THRASH
Being about things is what mind is about.

3-MINUTE THOUGHT
The traditional way of distinguishing mind and matter is to think of them as two distinct kinds of substance: physical stuff is solid, and has mass and extension; mental stuff has no weight or dimensions, but is a thing nonetheless. Dividing reality up into two radically different kinds of substance is problematic for many reasons (e.g. how do they interact?). Distinguishing the mental from the physical by means of intentionality, making no assumptions about substance, is therefore a tantalizing alternative.

What distinguishes the mental from the physical? According to Franz Brentano, the mark of the mental is that it is always directed at something other than itself, whereas physical things just are. Thoughts are *about* something, perceptions are *of* things, we make judgments about things, and loving or hating involves adopting an attitude towards the object of our emotions. For example, your thought that London is east of New York is about the two cities. Brentano said that physical things are never *about* or *of* things in this way: a rock isn't about anything, it just exists. It is true that expressions in a language, paintings, maps and so on can be about other things, but this kind of aboutness is something that is mind-created and mind-dependent, so it too is ultimately mental. This *aboutness* of the mental Brentano called 'intentionality'. There do seem to be some exceptions, what we might call 'raw feels'. For instance, a pain is surely not about or of anything, it just is. But for Brentano, pain still has an intentional aspect: pains represent damaged areas of the body. Most contemporary philosophers accept that intentionality is a mark of the mental, and that it is ultimately based in the brain and its activities. Exactly how this works is the 64-billion-dollar philosophical question.

RELATED PHILOSOPHIES
see also
DESCARTES' MIND-BODY PROBLEM
page 56

LAPLACE'S DEMON, DETERMINISM & FREE WILL
page 74

3-SECOND BIOGRAPHY
FRANZ BRENTANO
1838–1917

30-SECOND TEXT
Julian Baggini

Unintentional it may be, but thinking too hard about intentionality can make your brain hurt – or is it actually your mind that is sore?

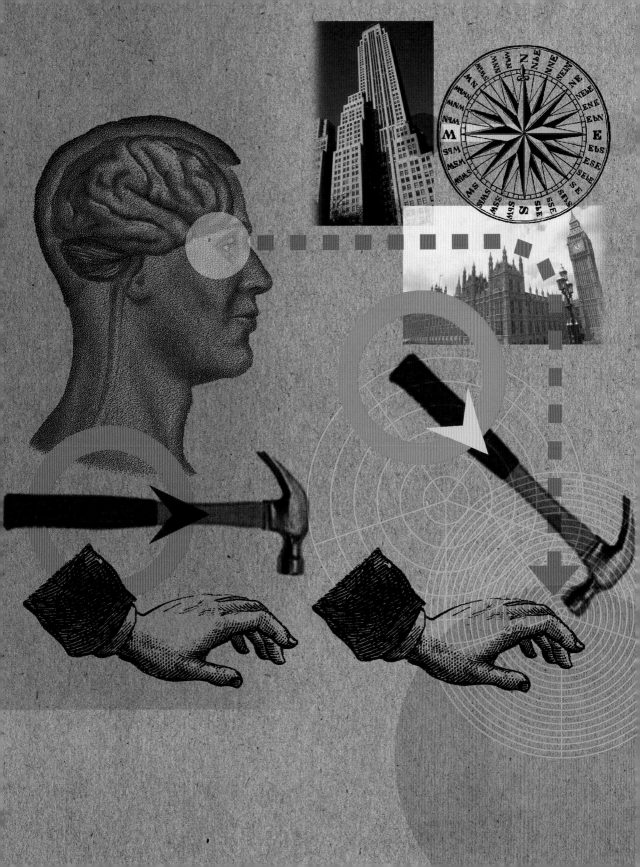

FODOR'S LANGUAGE OF THOUGHT

the 30-second philosophy

3-SECOND THRASH
Unbeknown to most of us we are expert users (though not speakers) of the language Mentalese.

3-MINUTE THOUGHT
Recent research on the psychology of infants has made a compelling case for the view that newborns come into the world already equipped with a lot of innate knowledge. For example, they know the difference between living and non-living things. Can it be that an infant already has the term in Mentalese that means 'elephant', before he ever sees an elephant? Fodor merely claims that there are words of Mentalese that are primed to refer to elephants when appropriate conditions are satisfied, and these conditions might involve seeing elephants or pictures of elephants.

The philosopher Jerry Fodor developed a controversial theory of the mind. He theorizes that there is an innate language of thought that he calls 'Mentalese'. He posited Mentalese in order to explain the nature of thinking (and other mental abilities), and to account for the learning of natural languages. Perceptions, memories and intentions all involve tokens of Mentalese sentences. So, when you think the thought that Kermit is green, a Mentalese sentence that means 'Kermit is green' occurs in your brain. Thoughts can be about objects (e.g. Kermit), and can be true or false because sentences are the kinds of things that can be about objects and be true or false. Mentalese sentences are like natural language sentences, in that they have grammatical structure, but they are different in that they are not used to communicate, but to think. Mentalese occurs prior to natural language. According to Fodor, learning a natural language such as English presupposes an existing ability to think in Mentalese. When we learn the meaning of a word, we learn to associate it with a Mentalese word. Mentalese is itself innate, although the ability to employ a Mentalese term may be triggered by having certain experiences. Fodor goes on to liken both conscious and unconscious mental activities to the operations of a computer. Thinking, perceiving and the rest involve computations with Mentalese sentences.

RELATED PHILOSOPHIES
see also
KANT'S SYNTHETIC *A PRIORI*
page 130

3-SECOND BIOGRAPHY
JERRY FODOR
1935–

30-SECOND TEXT
Kati Balog

She doesn't know what those animals are called in English – she hasn't learned that yet – but she's always known what they are in Mentalese.

PARFIT'S PERSONS

the 30-second philosophy

The contemporary philosopher

Derek Parfit asked the question, 'What makes a person the same person over time?' The question has also been asked by John Locke, who imagined a prince and a pauper exchanging memories, desires and other mental attributes. Locke said that the person who up till then had inhabited the prince's body would now inhabit the pauper's body, and the pauper-person would inhabit the prince's body. His view is that a person at one time and a person at a later time are the same person by virtue of the later person having the memories of and being mentally continuous with the earlier person. The police use fingerprints to identify a person, but if Locke is right this might be a mistake. Parfit continues Locke's discussion by imagining a person, say Captain Kirk, who steps into a faulty teleporter and is beamed to Earth where two Captains emerge, each with Kirk's memories, desires etc. Both of these have equal claim to be identical to Kirk, but are clearly not identical to each other. Parfit concludes that identity doesn't consist in memories and mental continuity. But he goes on to claim that this doesn't matter, since what we really care about is surviving, and survival consists in mental continuity.

RELATED PHILOSOPHIES
see also
CHALMER'S ZOMBIES
page 66

KANT'S LEFT HAND
page 70

THESEUS' SHIP
page 72

3-SECOND BIOGRAPHIES
DEREK PARFIT
1942–

JOHN LOCKE
1632–1704

30-SECOND TEXT
Kati Balog

3-SECOND THRASH
If you step into a teleporter and two of you come out, which one is you?

3-MINUTE THOUGHT
It may strike you that examples having to do with body-swapping princes and paupers, and multiple Captain Kirks are too fanciful to worry about. Philosophers are interested in these imaginary stories because they can help us understand our concept of a person. There may also be consequences for practical questions about punishment, particularly if an individual committed a crime in his youth, but has no memories of his earlier life and who, perhaps, is no longer the same person at all.

A person is the sum of his or her hopes, fears and past memories; nothing else really matters – but try telling that to the pauper.

1596
Born, La Haye, near
Tours, France

1616
Graduates in Law,
University of Poitiers

1628
Leaves for Holland, which
is to be his home until
1649

1637
Publishes *Discourse on
Method, with Optics,
Meteorology and
Geometry*

1641
*Meditations on First
Philosophy* is published
together with the first
six sets of *Objections
and Replies*

1644
*The Principles of
Philosophy* is published

1650
Dies, probably from
pneumonia

RENÉ DESCARTES

It is perhaps an oversimplification

to say that there were two major currents that shaped Descartes' life and work – the emergence of modern science as exemplified in the work of Copernicus and Galileo; and his realization that the Jesuit schooling he had received, which had promised so much, had delivered so little in terms of reliable knowledge. Nevertheless, it is the case that both these things were tremendously important in leading Descartes to develop the scientific and philosophical ideas that, in a sense, ushered in the modern world.

René Descartes was born in 1596 in La Haye, France, entered Jesuit College at the age of 11, and then studied Law at the University of Poitiers. However, rather than taking up a law career, Descartes went travelling and joined the army, which led to a chance meeting with the Dutch philosopher and scientist, Isaac Beeckman, which changed the course of his life. Their friendship sparked Descartes' interest in the sciences and set him on the path that eventually would make him the first great modern philosopher.

His major philosophical works were written in a 20-year period beginning in 1629. In *Discourse on Method*, published in 1637, originally as the preface to works on geometry, optics and meteorology, Descartes laid down the foundations of his epistemology and metaphysics. He followed this up in 1641 with the publication of his *Meditations on First Philosophy*, in which he articulated his famous method of doubt as a technique to establish the foundations of indubitable knowledge.

By the time of Descartes' death in 1650, his reputation for brilliance was well established. His ideas were being taught in Dutch universities; his *Meditations* had included critical contributions from luminaries such as John Locke; and he was well established in the finest intellectual circles of Europe. His legacy, though, has surpassed even these auspicious beginnings. It is fair to say that it is Descartes' work, more than that of any other philosopher, that has shaped the course of philosophy in the modern era.

CHALMERS' ZOMBIES

the 30-second philosophy

3-SECOND THRASH
No matter how much you know about the physical composition of the person sitting next to you, she may be a zombie.

3-MINUTE THOUGHT
Chalmers' view is a kind of dualism, since it says that consciousness is not physical. But unlike René Descartes, Chalmers doesn't think that there are mental substances. His view, rather, is that consciousness is a non-physical feature of certain physical things, and, in particular, of human brains. Most philosophers who uphold physicalism disagree with Chalmers, and claim that although the zombie scenario is non-contradictory, it doesn't follow that zombies are metaphysically possible.

David Chalmers recently revived arguments for dualism of mind and body by arguing that zombies are metaphysically possible. By 'zombie' he means beings that physically resemble conscious people but who are, nevertheless, not at all conscious. Since zombies are physically like conscious humans, they behave just like conscious humans. When your zombie twin steps on a nail it shouts 'Ouch!', but it feels nothing at all. Chalmers' argument for dualism begins with the thought that a zombie universe is conceivable. There is no contradiction in the scenario in which there is a universe that is physically just like ours in all respects, except that the creatures in it are completely devoid of consciousness. If this is correct, then consciousness is quite different from other biological phenomena, since there is a contradiction in thinking of a universe physically like ours where your zombie twin doesn't breathe, digest, reproduce and so on, exactly as you do. It follows from the conceivability of the zombie scenario, claims Chalmers, that zombies are a genuine metaphysical possibility. If zombies are metaphysically possible, and we are conscious, then there is more in our Universe than physical entities, and things composed entirely of physical entities, and certain arrangements. There is also non-physical consciousness!

RELATED PHILOSOPHIES
see also
PARFIT'S PERSONS
page 62

3-SECOND BIOGRAPHY
DAVID CHALMERS
1966–

30-SECOND TEXT
Kati Balog

One thinks, therefore he exists, while the other cannot think, but he exists as well. What's the difference between them exactly?

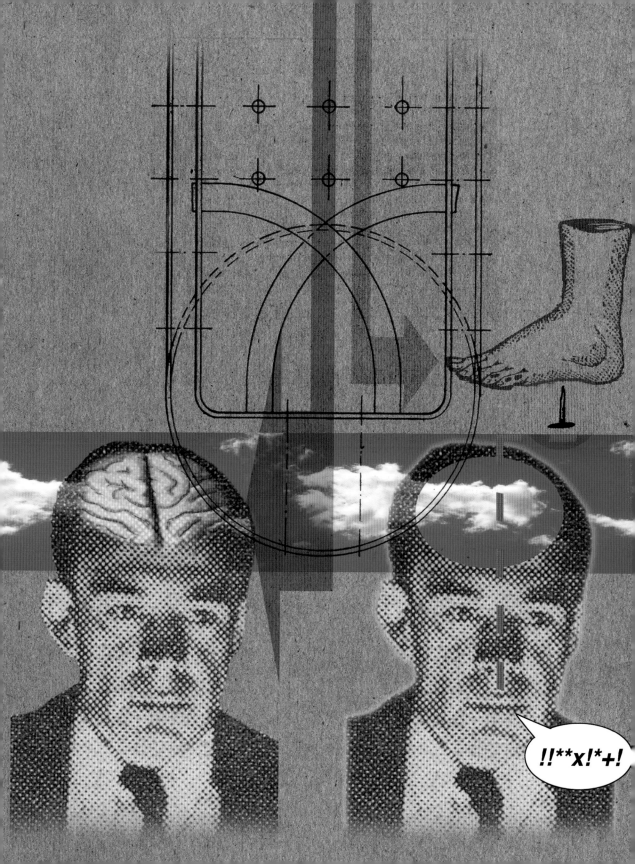

ZENO'S PARADOXES

the 30-second philosophy

The ancient Greek philosopher, Zeno of Elea, conceived of many paradoxes of time and motion. For instance, logically it can be argued that if Achilles gives a tortoise a head start in a race, then he could never overtake it, as long as the tortoise keeps moving. This is because in order to first overtake it, he must reach where the tortoise is, but by the time he gets there, the tortoise will have moved on. So, Achilles must then reach where the tortoise has moved on to, but once he gets there, the tortoise has already gone, and so on, ad infinitum. Another paradox states that an arrow can never move, since in any given moment of time, the arrow had to completely occupy a certain space. Like a photograph, at any given moment, the arrow is where it is and not somewhere else. Hence it is stationary. But if time is no more than a series of moments, and if the arrow is stationary at every particular moment, it never moves. Yet we know that arrows do move, and that Achilles can overtake the tortoise. So what is flawed – our view of reality, or the logic of the paradoxes?

3-SECOND BIOGRAPHY
ZENO
490–430 BCE

30-SECOND TEXT
Julian Baggini

3-SECOND THRASH
It may not be better to travel than to arrive, but at least it's possible.

3-MINUTE THOUGHT
The key to solving the paradoxes is to look at what they assume: that time is a series of static moments (the arrow), or that space and time can be divided up into ever smaller chunks (the tortoise). In order to generate the puzzles, we have to assume certain things about the nature of time and space. Zeno's paradoxes draw out these assumptions, and make us question them.

Zeno's motion paradoxes had the ancient world running hard just to stay still. But, without the questions posed by the paradoxes, physicists would not have gotten the modern world on the move by explaining the nature of space, time and matter.

KANT'S LEFT HAND

the 30-second philosophy

3-SECOND THRASH
Newton said: 'Space is absolute'; Leibniz said: 'There are only spatial relations'; and Kant handed the victory to Newton!

3-MINUTE THOUGHT
The debate between absolutists and relationists about space continues to this day. Relationists reply to Kant that his thought experiment is misleading. He is really imagining a universe with more than a left (or right) hand in it. He is imagining himself in the universe looking at the hand, and that is enough for the relationist to find distance relations that distinguish left from right. Some physicists claim that the laws of nature themselves require an absolute distinction between left and right to account for the decays of certain particles.

Immanuel Kant thought long and hard about a dispute between Isaac Newton and Gottfried Leibniz. Newton claimed that space was a kind of theatre (he called it 'God's sensorium') in which locations are absolute. It followed that, had God placed all the particles in the Universe 160 kilometres (100 miles) from their present locations while keeping their distances the same, he would have made a different Universe. Leibniz thought this was absurd. He said that God would have no reason to put the particles in one place rather than another. Instead, he said that space is not a place, but rather that space consists of relations of distance between particles. Kant thought he could prove Newton right and Leibniz wrong with a thought experiment. He imagined a universe in which there existed nothing but a left hand, and a different universe in which there was nothing but a right hand. All of the relations between all of the particles that made up the hand were exactly the same in the two cases. They were mirror images (look at the picture!). Kant argued that since the two situations were obviously different, space was more than distance relations between particles. Leibniz is wrong, and Newton is right!

RELATED PHILOSOPHIES
see also
PARFIT'S PERSONS
page 62

3-SECOND BIOGRAPHY
IMMANUEL KANT
1724–1804

30-SECOND TEXT
Barry Loewer

Everyone who agrees with Kant please raise your hand? Left or right, it doesn't matter – or does it?

THESEUS' SHIP

the 30-second philosophy

Theseus' ship is put into dry

dock. Bit by bit, each part of it is replaced. As one old board is torn out, a new one is put in. Eventually, the work is complete, and the ship sets sail. However, someone has been collecting all the old bits and has put them back together again, and this ship too goes to sea. So, which of these two vessels is the real ship of Theseus? The one made of the original material, you might say. But that's not what Theseus thinks: he believes his ship has been renovated, not replaced. Nor is it the case that we always think that ownership is a matter of a particular physical thing: when Paddington Bear went to the bank to withdraw five pounds and reported, stunned, that the note he was given was not his one, he misunderstood the nature of money. This problem, set by Thomas Hobbes, might seem very abstract, but consider for a moment that every cell in your body changes over time. So, are people particular lumps of matter, or a continuous way of organizing matter that is always changing? Are we like banknotes, or monetary value?

RELATED PHILOSOPHIES
see also
PARFIT'S PERSONS
page 62

3-SECOND BIOGRAPHY
THOMAS HOBBES
1588–1679

30-SECOND TEXT
Julian Baggini

3-SECOND THRASH
Have you changed, or have you been changed for someone else?

3-MINUTE THOUGHT
Think of the puzzle in terms of types and tokens. Tokens are particular physical objects, whereas types are forms of objects that may be instantiated in different tokens. So, for example, it doesn't matter what tokens (particular notes) your money comes in, as long as the type (value) is the same. Would it matter if your spouse was replaced by an identical token? If so, why? Do you love those particular atoms?

Ownership is nine tenths of the law – but 100 percent of the material in Theseus' ship has been replaced. Is it still his ship? You do the maths.

LAPLACE'S DEMON, DETERMINISM & FREE WILL

the 30-second philosophy

Pierre-Simon Laplace supposed

that everything is composed of atoms and that the motions of atoms are governed by the laws that Isaac Newton discovered in the 17th century. Laplace imagined a super intelligent and mathematically gifted demon, who knows the positions and velocities of all particles in the Universe at a particular time, along with all the laws of nature. He claimed that this demon could compute the positions and velocities of all particles at every other time. The demon could predict where your body would be, and how it would be moving next year from its knowledge of the positions and velocities of the particles in the Universe a million years ago. Laplace's argument depends on the fact that Newton's laws are deterministic. Many philosophers have concluded that determinism is incompatible with free will. For, if the motions of your body are determined by what happened a million years ago, how can it be 'up to you' whether you, say, raise your left hand? They conclude that either determinism is false, or free will is an illusion. Other philosophers claim that to have free will it is sufficient to have intentional control over whether you raise your left hand and that, such control is compatible with determinism.

RELATED PHILOSOPHIES
see also
DESCARTE'S MIND-BODY PROBLEM
page 56

BRENTANO'S INTENTIONALITY
page 58

LUCRETIUS' ATOMISM
page 58

SARTRE'S BAD FAITH
page 152

3-SECOND BIOGRAPHY
PIERRE-SIMON LAPLACE
1749–1827

30-SECOND TEXT
Kati Balog

3-SECOND THRASH
Laplace's demon calculates the way your body will move tomorrow from the positions of particles in the past, thereby depriving you of free will.

3-MINUTE THOUGHT
It is commonly thought that current physics tells us that the fundamental laws of quantum mechanics are not deterministic but just tell us probabilities. Some philosophers think that this solves the problem of free will. But it is controversial to say that quantum mechanics is not deterministic, and even if its laws are probabilistic, they might not allow for free will.

Does free will exist? If not, can we have such things as justice or morals? We could ask Laplace's demon, but he might be just as uncertain about it as we are.

RYLE'S GHOST IN THE MACHINE
the 30-second philosophy

3-SECOND THRASH
The way to solve the mind-body problem is to exorcise the ghost in the machine.

3-MINUTE THOUGHT
Ryle's view of the mind is a sophisticated version of behaviourism. His idea is that a sentence attributing a mental state or process to a person really means that this person behaves or is disposed to behave in certain ways. While this may have some plausibility for certain sentences, such as 'She is inquisitive', it is very implausible for sentences such as 'She is thinking about philosophy', and 'She is feeling a cool breeze on her cheeks'.

The 20th-century philosopher

Gilbert Ryle said that philosophers (and ordinary folk) who think of the mind as a kind of thing that causes the body to move are making a bad mistake. He called this view of the mind 'the ghost in the machine', and he attributed it to René Descartes. He called this type of mistake a 'category mistake'. Someone who, having been taken around all of Oxford's buildings said, 'I see all these buildings, but where is Oxford?' would be making a category mistake, the mistake of thinking that Oxford is in the same category as the other buildings. He doesn't understand that the buildings are parts of Oxford. Ryle claimed that those who think of the mind as a thing in addition to the body are missing the point that the body and its activities comprise the mind. Ryle's view is that when we say that Hillary has an inquisitive mind, we are not saying that there is some thing associated with Hillary's body, namely, her mind, which is inquisitive and causes to make her inquisitive remarks. Instead, we mean that Hillary behaves in inquisitive ways. The mind is not a ghost in the machine, but rather a way of describing the machine's activities.

RELATED PHILOSOPHIES
see also
DESCARTES' MIND-BODY PROBLEM
page 56

BRENTANO'S INTENTIONALITY
page 58

3-SECOND BIOGRAPHY
GILBERT RYLE
1900–1976

30-SECOND TEXT
Kati Balog

According to Gilbert Ryle, he thinks, therefore he is, but all he is, is the manifestation of an unconscious, physical process.

ETHICS & POLITICAL PHILOSOPHY

ETHICS & POLITICAL PHILOSOPHY
GLOSSARY

alienation The separation of aspects of the human world that ought to go together, according to Karl Marx, and several others. For Marx, for example, a worker loses something of himself by becoming merely another mindless part of a production line. He is separated from the satisfactions of work, and distanced from the fruits of his labour, among other things.

character A person's moral nature, the morally relevant parts of an individual's personality. For Aristotle, living a moral life amounts not only to doing what is right – as perhaps a utilitarian would have it – but also to cultivating a virtuous character, being a good person.

hedonism The view that the main aim or goal of life is pleasure. There are psychological hedonists who claim that humans only desire pleasure, and moral philosophers who claim that pleasure is what we ought to desire, that pleasure has moral value.

historical materialism The conception of human history as determined by, or dependent on, how human beings produce the material requirements of life, owed to Karl Marx and Friedrich Engels.

imperatives Immanuel Kant thought that imperatives, or rules for action, guide us in two ways. Hypothetical imperatives tell us what to do if we want to achieve some goal or other. Categorical imperatives tell us what to do, regardless of the consequences. For Kant, the demands of morality can only be categorical in nature.

mean The virtuous middle between two extremes. A virtuous character, for the Aristotelian, has something to do with action in the middle of two sorts of vices: excess on the one hand, and insufficiency on the other. For example, the virtuous person exhibits courage by observing the mean between the excess of rashness and the insufficiency of cowardice.

mode of production For Karl Marx, the way a society organizes and secures its basic needs, commodities, etc. The mode of production is an enormous web of workers, tools, raw materials and general socio-economic relations which, he thought, has a substantial bearing on the sort of life, the sort of 'consciousness', characteristic of every age.

moral intuitions The inner responses that can nudge one towards the conclusion that an action, or person or the like is morally right or wrong. Philosophers are sometimes guided by their moral intuitions when trying to adjudicate between competing moral theories.

noble savage A human being unspoilt by the corrupting influences of government and society, as envisioned by Jean-Jacques Rousseau, and others. The noble savage is peaceful, innocent and possessed of a kind of natural dignity, as opposed to the violent brutes imagined by Thomas Hobbes.

social contract An agreement, implicit or otherwise, imagined by political philosophers in an effort to explain the connection between political obligation, the consent of the governed and the power of the state.

state of nature An imagined time before or without government. Some political theorists speculate about the state of nature in an effort to work out what government is for by trying to think of human beings living without it.

ARISTOTLE'S ETHICS

the 30-second philosophy

3-SECOND THRASH
There is no dark and bright side of the force, but rather two dark ends and a light middle.

3-MINUTE THOUGHT
Aristotle's approach to ethics has been revived in recent decades, under the name of 'virtue ethics'. One challenge it faces is over the central importance of character. The worry is that the idea is circular: we know what the right thing to do is because that's what a person of good character would do; but how do you know whether a person has good moral character? Because of what they do ...?

Aristotle's first rule for being good is that there are no rules. Being good is about developing your character, so that you are disposed to do the best thing in each situation. It is not about internalizing some moral manual. Human beings are creatures of habit and, just as a good musician becomes so by practising, so, by doing virtuous things, we become virtuous people. But what is virtue? It is living according to our natures as rational animals. A good dog does doggy things well, and a good person does human things well, especially thinking, because this is the one thing we can do that no other living thing can. We can be guided towards right action by surrendering the idea that good and bad are opposites, and instead thinking of the good as lying on a 'mean' between the extremes of excess and deficiency. For instance, courage lies between the excess of rashness and the deficiency of cowardice; generosity between meanness and profligacy; kindness between the excess of disregard for others and the deficiency of indulgence. Contrary to how morality is often conceived, Aristotle's ethics are about more than being good – they are a blueprint for living well.

RELATED PHILOSOPHIES
see also
STATES OF NATURE & THE SOCIAL CONTRACT
page 84

3-SECOND BIOGRAPHY
ARISTOTLE
384–322 BC

30-SECOND TEXT
Julian Baggini

Doing the right thing is not just about following rules, but striking the correct balance, according to the circumstances in which you find yourself – both good and bad.

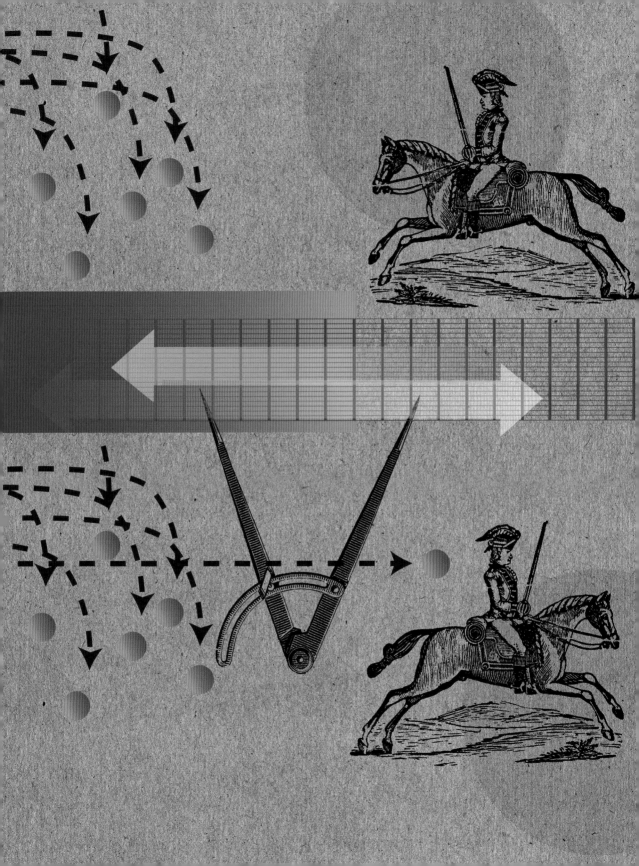

STATES OF NATURE & THE SOCIAL CONTRACT

the 30-second philosophy

3-SECOND THRASH
If you think humans are corrupt and depraved, and that we rub along because of the civilizing effect of society, then you're with Hobbes; if you think our nature is basically noble, but that we are corrupted by malign social forces, then you're with Rousseau.

3-MINUTE THOUGHT
Most modern forms of conservatism are broadly Hobbesian – conservatives tend to be suspicious of the claim that it is possible to create more harmonious societies by changing existing political and social arrangements. Left-wing thought, in contrast, is more sanguine. Most socialists are attracted by the idea that if you get society right, you'll also get people right.

Thomas Hobbes and Jean-Jacques Rousseau had very different ideas about the essential nature of human beings. Hobbes argued that without the civilizing effect of society, lives would be solitary, poor, nasty, brutish and short, lived in continual fear, and with the danger of violent death. Rousseau, in contrast, was much more optimistic: in a state of nature, human beings are 'noble savages', who live a solitary, peaceful existence, concerned mainly with the satisfaction of their immediate needs. This difference is reflected in the way that each of these two men saw civil and political society. For Hobbes, civilization is a precondition of worthwhile lives. It is only by signing up to a 'social contract', and thereby transferring some of our natural rights to an absolute authority (a Leviathan), that it is possible to avoid a war of all against all. Rousseau also thought a social contract necessary, but his reasoning was different. He argued that civilization is the original source of our problems. Property rights, enshrined in civil society, generate inequality, with all its attendant vices, inevitable. The only way to overcome the selfishness and moral depravity that is the consequence of civilization is for people to accept the authority of the 'general will' of the population.

RELATED PHILOSOPHIES
see also
ARISTOTLE'S ETHICS
page 82

MILL'S UTILITARIANISM
page 90

3-SECOND BIOGRAPHIES
THOMAS HOBBES
1588–1679

JEAN-JACQUES ROUSSEAU
1712–1778

30-SECOND TEXT
Jeremy Stangroom

Is monstrous behaviour natural or created by society? Perhaps the answer depends on whether society is part of, or separate from, nature.

KANT'S CATEGORICAL IMPERATIVE

the 30-second philosophy

RELATED PHILOSOPHIES
see also
MILL'S UTILITARIANISM
page 90

THE TROLLEY PROBLEM
page 94

3-SECOND BIOGRAPHY
IMMANUEL KANT
1724–1804

30-SECOND TEXT
James Garvey

3-SECOND THRASH
If your mother ever brought you in line by asking, 'What if everyone else did that?'– it turns out she's a Kantian.

3-MINUTE THOUGHT
One can see Kant's point, but still wonder what to do when your moral duties conflict. Suppose I see that breaking promises is wrong. Should I cut short the emergency medical assistance I am giving to someone because I promised to meet a friend for drinks? Does my duty to help someone in need override my duty to keep promises? Probably sometimes it does, but seeing why, in Kant's view, is not straightforward.

Consistency is at the heart of morality. If I think that I deserve a certain sort of treatment, then others in my situation are entitled to that treatment, too. The German philosopher Immanuel Kant argued that consistency is assured if we follow the categorical imperative: 'Act only according to that maxim by which you can, at the same time, wish that it should become a universal law.' If your rule or maxim could consistently be followed by everybody, then you are in no danger of doing wrong. Suppose you are thinking of borrowing money and promising to pay it back, when you know you can never do so. The rule you are thinking of following might be: 'Make a false promise if it furthers your interests.' If that rule were to become a universal law of nature, something followed automatically by everyone in your situation, would that world be a consistent (i.e. moral) one? Well, no one would believe a promise, so promising would be impossible and, therefore, you could not make a false promise in the first place. So, the rule you are considering is not in accordance with the moral law. Breaking promises is, therefore, wrong.

Is lying to the bank a good thing to do? The answer is no – otherwise the bank will think it is a good idea to lie to you, too.

1724
Born, Königsberg,
Prussia

1740
Enrols at the University
of Königsberg

1755
Begins lecturing at the
University

1755
Becomes Professor of
Logic and Metaphysics

1781
Critique of Pure Reason
published

1788
*Critique of Practical
Reason* published

1790
Critique of Judgment
published

1797
Retires from the
University

1804
Dies

IMMANUEL KANT

By the time he was 46,

Immanuel Kant was a Professor at the University of Königsberg, a renowned scholar, published in the field of astronomy, and gaining an burgeoning reputation as a philosopher. However, he spent the next decade in silent isolation, living a life of such regularity that it is said that the inhabitants of Königsberg were able to set their clocks by the timing of his afternoon walks. The result of this silent decade was the publication of the *Critique of Pure Reason* in 1781, generally considered one of the greatest works in the history of philosophy.

Kant was born in Königsberg, Prussia, in 1724, the fourth of eleven children born to Johann Georg Kant, a German craftsman, and Anna Regina Porter. He spent his entire life in Königsberg, never travelling more than 80 kilometres or so from his hometown. His schooling was unspectacular, but he did well enough to enroll at the University of Königsberg when he was 16. It was here that he was first introduced to philosophy, and he spent the next ten years studying and tutoring, before he became a professor at his alma mater in 1755.

The parochialism of Kant's life stands in stark contrast to the breadth of his philosophical concerns. In addition to the *Critique of Pure Reason*, which laid down the fundamentals of his epistemology and metaphysics, he wrote two brilliant works of moral philosophy, *Groundwork of the Metaphysics of Morals*, and the *Critique of Practical Reason*, published in 1785 and 1788 respectively, plus an important treatment of aesthetics, the *Critique of Judgment*, in 1790, his last major work.

The importance of Kant's work only properly came to be appreciated by his contemporaries towards the end of his life. However, by the time of his death in 1804, it was becoming apparent that his argument that the mind was actively involved in constituting the empirical world was going to turn out to be every bit the Copernican revolution in philosophy that he had claimed.

MILL'S UTILITARIANISM

the 30-second philosophy

3-SECOND THRASH
An action is right to
the extent that it tends
to promote happiness,
particularly if it is the
right kind of happiness.

3-MINUTE THOUGHT
There are many difficult
issues with utilitarianism.
Consider, for example,
that if an action is right
to the extent that it
promotes the greatest
happiness of the greatest
number of people, then
it might be justified to
torture a thief in a football
stadium if it meant that
the crowd went home
happy. Moreover, Mill's
arguments about higher
pleasures are suspect. The
fact that people who have
experienced both Mozart
and ice cream might prefer
Mozart doesn't seem
to be a moral argument,
but simply a matter of
individual taste.

The central claim of John Stuart
Mill's theory of utilitarianism is that actions are
right to the extent that they tend to promote
happiness, and wrong to the extent that they
produce unhappiness, where happiness means
pleasure and unhappiness means pain. A key
point here is that Mill is talking about aggregate
happiness, or the greatest happiness of the
greatest number of people. However, Mill was
not happy to leave this formulation as it stood,
since it allowed for the possibility that it might
be better to be spend one's life engaged in
hedonistic pursuits, rather than partaking of
the fruits of human civilization. Consequently,
he introduced the idea that certain kinds of
pleasure are better than others. Listening to
Mozart, for example, is likely a better kind of
pleasure than eating Ben & Jerry's ice cream.
He justified this contention by an appeal to
experience: nobody who has experienced both
higher and lower pleasures would be willing to
swap a life filled with the former for a life filled
with the latter. As he put it: 'No intelligent
human being would consent to be a fool ... even
though they should be persuaded that the fool,
the dunce or the rascal is better satisfied with
his lot than they are with theirs.'

RELATED PHILOSOPHIES
see also
KANT'S CATEGORICAL
IMPERATIVE
page 86

THE TROLLEY PROBLEM
page 94

3-SECOND BIOGRAPHY
JOHN STUART MILL
1806–1873

30-SECOND TEXT
Jeremy Stangroom

*According to John
Stuart Mill it is very
good to put on a
public performance
of Mozart – and it is
still okay to sell ice
cream in the interval.*

MARX'S HISTORICAL MATERIALISM

the 30-second philosophy

3-SECOND THRASH
The history of society
is the story of conflict
between great opposing
social forces (or classes),
which will only cease when
the workers of the world
rise up, throw off their
chains, and abolish the
capitalist system.

3-MINUTE THOUGHT
The Marxist idea that
capitalism will be replaced
by a society free of
systematic inequality
and conflict is not very
plausible in light of the
events of recent history.
Not only is capitalism
still going strong, but the
socialist experiments of the
20th century all ended in
failure. Moreover, Hitler's
concentration camps
and Stalin's gulags make
it hard to believe that
human beings will become
rational, and self-aware,
because the productive
forces of society are
collectively owned.

The foundational premise of
Karl Marx's historical materialism is that the
form that society takes is determined by the
way in which production is organized. This has
meant a fundamental division between those
who own and control the means of production
(factories, machinery, tools and the like) and
those who do not. Marx claimed that the
conflict between the 'haves' and the 'have
nots' has been the motor of history. The most
advanced mode of organizing production is
capitalism. It is characterized by the existence
of two great classes: the bourgeoisie, the
owners of the means of production; and the
proletariat, who own only their own labour
power. The proletariat are forced to sell their
labour to the bourgeoisie in order to survive.
They expend their productive energy for the
benefit of the class that exploits them. This
dynamic renders capitalism unstable. The
proletariat, aware of the reality of its situation,
can rise up and overthrow the existing system.
Marx argued that it is inevitable that capitalism
will eventually collapse under the weight of its
own contradictions. The historical destiny of the
proletariat is to institute a new form of society
– communism – based on collective ownership.
In doing so, they will end the alienation of the
proletariat from the labour process itself, and
from their essential humanity.

RELATED PHILOSOPHIES
see also
KANT'S CATEGORICAL
IMPERATIVE
page 86

MILL'S UTILITARIANISM
page 90

3-SECOND BIOGRAPHY
KARL MARX
1818–1883

30-SECOND TEXT
Jeremy Stangroom

*According to Marx,
the bourgeoisie will
continue to raise
their glasses to
the hard-working
proletariat until the
revolution comes.*

THE TROLLEY PROBLEM

the 30-second philosophy

RELATED PHILOSOPHIES
see also
KANT'S CATEGORICAL IMPERATIVE
page 86

MILL'S UTILITARIANISM
page 90

3-SECOND THRASH
If it is okay to divert a trolley so that it runs over one person rather than five people, why is it not okay to push a passer-by in front of a trolley in order to save the lives of the same five people?

3-MINUTE THOUGHT
Two things seem to be involved in our responses to these scenarios. First, if we divert the trolley we are not doing something directly to the man tied to the track as we would be if we pushed the man off the bridge. Secondly, the man tied to the track is already involved in the events, whereas the man on the bridge is not. Neither explanation is particularly satisfactory; our responses to this problem probably have more to do with human psychology than strictly moral reasoning.

The trolley problem is a thought experiment designed to tell us something about our moral intuitions. First articulated by Philippa Foot, its basic form is as follows: a trolley (railway carriage) is running out of control down a track. In its path are five people who are tied to the track. Happily, it is possible to flip a switch that will send the trolley down a different track to safety. Unfortunately, there's one person tied to that track who will be killed if you flip the switch. What should you do? Most people say that it is right to flip the switch. If you're committed to utilitarian ethics, where an action is right to the extent that it increases the general happiness, it seems that you are duty bound to change the course of the trolley. However, Judith Jarvis Thompson suggests an interesting variation on the trolley problem, which shows that our utilitarian intuitions are not wholly reliable. The scenario is the same, except this time you're standing on a bridge under which the trolley will pass, and there's a large man standing next to you. The only way to save the five people is to push him onto the track, thereby stopping the trolley. Is this the right thing to do? The moral calculus seems similar: one person is sacrificed to save five. But this time the moral intuition is different: people tend to think that it would be wrong to push the man off the bridge.

3-SECOND BIOGRAPHIES
PHILIPPA FOOT
1920–

JUDITH JARVIS THOMPSON
1929–

30-SECOND TEXT
Jeremy Stangroom

It looks like a rail crash is about to happen. What are you going to do? Whatever you decide, it's going to end badly.

RELIGION

agnostic An individual who suspends judgment on the question of the existence of God, perhaps because of equal evidence on both sides of the question.

all-good A godly attribute variously understood as being perfectly good, just or loving. There are questions, first raised by Socrates, to do with the relationship between goodness and God's goodness. Is what is morally right commanded by God because it's morally right, or is it morally right because God commands it? Either possibility is unsatisfactory for the theist.

all-knowing A godly attribute variously understood as knowing all truths, knowing everything, having access to all true propositions, knowing everything that can be known, etc. There are implications for human freedom, for, if God is omniscient, then presumably He knows what any of us might do before we do it.

all-powerful A godly attribute variously understood as being able to do anything, being able to do anything that it is logically possible to do, being able to do anything in line with God's nature, etc. There are questions associated with incoherence, for example, can God create a stone so heavy that He cannot lift it? There are also problems associated with there being any limits on God's power, given his goodness.

atheist An individual who denies the existence of God.

design A property detected in natural objects by those who argue for the existence of God. If the parts of an object exhibit a certain sort of organization – seem to 'conspire together to achieve a purpose' – then some conclude that there is an intelligence, perhaps a Divine Intelligence, behind the existence of the object.

evil Philosophical shorthand for suffering. Even though 'evil' usually refers to nefarious human activity, the word as used in debates about God refers to pain and suffering generally, and sometimes to the cause of suffering. A headache is a kind of evil, in this usage. The existence of evil is a problem for theism.

God A monotheistic deity, the subject of philosophical reflection bound up with the Western, Judaeo-Christian tradition. God, as conceived philosophically, is thought to be the all-knowing, all-powerful and all-good creator of the Universe, possibly also the arbiter of right and wrong. The philosophy of religion takes up arguments for and against the existence of God, the characterization of God's nature, the epistemology of belief in God, along with much else.

intelligent design A contemporary movement predicated on a very old philosophical argument for God's existence called 'the teleological argument' (from the ancient Greek *telos*, meaning goal or end). Modern thinkers call it 'the argument from design'. Objections are legion.

miracle According to David Hume, a miracle is a violation of a law of nature by the intervention of God. A comparison of the evidence for belief in a miracle on the one hand, and belief in a law of nature on the other, forms the basis of his scepticism about miracles generally.

ontological Of or having to do with being, with what exists. The ontological argument for God's existence tries to show that existence is simply built into the concept of God.

theist An individual who believes that God exists.

AQUINAS' FIVE WAYS

the 30-second philosophy

3-SECOND THRASH
Reflect on the existence of certain undeniable features of our world, and you will conclude that God's existence is undeniable, too.

3-MINUTE THOUGHT
One of the five ways still gets a hearing – the argument from design. Proponents of intelligent design note the order in nature. Eyes seem built for vision, wings seem built for flight, and so on. Critics long before Darwin have replied, partly, by pointing to the Universe's many design flaws. Whose idea was it, anyway, to have us breathe and drink through the same pipe? A minor adjustment would avoid a lot of choking.

Saint Thomas Aquinas is one of the first thinkers in the Western, theistic tradition to use empirical evidence to persuade non-believers of the existence of God. The five ways are five proofs of the existence of God, and each one begins with some truth about the world that is difficult for an non-believer to deny. Aquinas then argues backwards from that truth to the existence of God. For example, you might have noticed that many of the things around you are moving. Whatever moves was moved by something else which also moves – nothing just spontaneously moves itself. Aquinas thought that this chain of moving things could not go back indefinitely. Movement would become stalled in an infinite regress, and nothing would be moving now. Plainly, things are moving, so there must be some first, Unmoved Mover back there that sets the whole chain in motion. This, Aquinas concludes, can only be God. The other four arguments proceed in much the same way. For example, thoughts about the fact that all events have a cause lead back to an Uncaused Cause, which gets the whole causal ball rolling, while reflection on degrees of perfection leads back to the existence of a Perfect Being.

RELATED PHILOSOPHIES
see also
ANSELM'S ONTOLOGICAL ARGUMENT
page 102

3-SECOND BIOGRAPHY
SAINT THOMAS AQUINAS
1224/25–1274

30-SECOND TEXT
James Garvey

Someone had to set the balls rolling, didn't they?

ANSELM'S ONTOLOGICAL ARGUMENT

the 30-second philosophy

RELATED PHILOSOPHIES
see also
AQUINAS' FIVE WAYS
page 100

3-SECOND BIOGRAPHY
ANSELM OF CANTERBURY
1033–1109

30-SECOND TEXT
Jeremy Stangroom

3-SECOND THRASH
If God existed only in the mind, He wouldn't be much of a God; since a God who isn't much of a God isn't a God, He must exist in reality as well.

3-MINUTE THOUGHT
Anselm's ontological proof has provoked a massive literature. This is not surprising, since the argument is simultaneously beguiling, yet surely false. One of the earliest criticisms of it was voiced by the monk Gaunilo, a contemporary of Anselm, who showed that a similar argument could be employed for any entity: We can conceive of a perfect chair. A perfect chair must be more perfect in reality than in the mind. Therefore, a perfect chair exists. Probably, though, it won't be on sale at IKEA.

Anselm of Canterbury, later Saint Anselm, believed that by using reason alone it is possible to show that God exists, that the human soul is immortal and that scripture is without error. Most of the arguments he employed to this end no longer hold any interest. However, his ontological proof of God remains a live issue in modern philosophy. It runs like this: (1) God is defined as 'that than which nothing greater can be conceived'. (2) It is possible for things that exist in the mind – for example, the idea of God – also to exist in reality. There are then two possibilities here: God exists only in the mind, or God exists in the mind and in reality. (3) If something exists in the mind and in reality, it is greater than anything that exists solely in the mind. (4) We have defined God as 'that than which nothing greater can be conceived'. However, if God exists only in the mind, we can conceive of something greater, namely a God which exists in the mind and reality. Therefore, God cannot exist just in the mind. (5) Hey presto! It follows that God exists – both in the mind, and in reality.

If God didn't exist we'd have to invent him—and as soon as we do, we'd bring God into existence.

1224
Born, Roccasecca, near Naples

1231
Enters school at the abbey at Monte Cassino

1239
Begins studies at the University of Naples

1244
Joins the Dominican Order

1250
Ordained as a priest

1252
Enters the University of Paris to complete a Masters degree

1262
Completes his masterpiece *Summa contra Gentiles*

1270–3
Work progresses on *Summa Theologiae*

1273
Suddenly stops work on *Summa Theologiae*

1274
Dies on his way to attend the Second Council of Lyon

THOMAS AQUINAS

In 1244, at the age of 20, Thomas Aquinas, who would later be canonized and celebrated as one of history's greatest theologians, joined the Order of Dominican friars, which promptly commanded that he leave his native Italy for Paris, where he would be able to continue with his studies. This rather annoyed his large, aristocratic family, who had hoped that he would become the abbot of Monte Cassino. So they arranged for him to be kidnapped while en route, and then dragged him back to his hometown, Roccasecca, near Naples, where they imprisoned him for more than a year. However, he was eventually allowed to return to the Dominicans, and then travel on to Paris, after he had demonstrated his piety by chasing away a prostitute that his brother had hired in order to tempt him from his godly path.

From Paris, Aquinas moved to Cologne, where he was ordained as a priest, before returning to Paris to begin a Master of Theology degree at the university. In 1256 he qualified, and became a teacher at the university. Aquinas spent most of the remainder of his life travelling between the learned institutions of France and Italy. Although he died while still only in his forties, he produced a staggeringly large body of work – many millions of words, all told.

This avalanche of words, which resulted in such masterpieces as *Summa contra Gentiles* and *Summa Theologiae*, stopped abruptly following Mass on the Feast of St Nicholas in 1273, with Aquinas declaring, 'All that I have written seems to me like straw compared to what has now been revealed to me'. A few months later, while on his way to a church council meeting, he managed to bash his head on an overhanging branch and fall off his donkey. He died shortly afterwards in the Cistercian Abbey at Fossanova.

EPICURUS' RIDDLE

the 30-second philosophy

It is possible to come to the conclusion that the existence of evil is incompatible with the existence of an all-knowing, all-powerful and all-good God. If anything has to give, it's the existence of God, because what we cannot deny is the fact of evil in the world. Perhaps the first formulation of this, the so-called 'problem of evil' for theism, is owed to the ancient Greek philosopher Epicurus. We don't know exactly what Epicurus said – all we have to go on are the reports of ancient commentators – but we do know that Epicurus was not arguing for atheism, exactly. His general aim was to remove fear from human lives, and a large source of fear in his day was fear of the gods. You never knew when you might be in for a good smiting. But, given the existence of evil (or, better, undeserved evil), it looked like the gods did not really have much to do with human lives. The riddle runs, roughly, like this: either the gods want to do something about evil, and cannot, or they can, but do not. So, they're either impotent, and therefore nothing to worry about, or wicked, and therefore not really gods.

3-SECOND THRASH
Why do bad things happen to good people?

3-MINUTE THOUGHT
There are many theistic replies to the problem of evil. Some argue that the evil which exists is somehow necessary, a crucial part of God's divine plan. Perhaps God put a bit of evil in the world to test us, to give us a chance to choose to be virtuous. Others point out that some evil is overwhelming, a test we can't help but fail. Anyway, couldn't God have just made us virtuous in the first place?

3-SECOND BIOGRAPHY
EPICURUS
341–270 BC

30-SECOND TEXT
James Garvey

How can righteous gods allow evil to exist? That's a good question, but be polite when you ask them, in case they turn nasty.

PALEY'S WATCHMAKER

the 30-second philosophy

RELATED PHILOSOPHIES
see also
ANSELM'S ONTOLOGICAL
ARGUMENT
page 102

AQUINAS' FIVE WAYS
page 100

3-SECOND THRASH
Common sense comes up
against Darwin – and loses.

3-MINUTE THOUGHT
Intelligent design theorists
use a more sophisticated
version of Paley's
argument. They argue
that particular features
of particular organisms
could not have evolved
by chance, and thus the
best explanation for their
existence is divine design.
To say that intelligent
design is controversial is
true, but to say science
is divided on the issue
is misleading. There are
two camps, but almost
all biologists think the
evidence greatly favours
natural selection over
intelligent design as
an explanation for the
diversity and complexity
of life on Earth.

Imagine you are walking along a beach and you come across a watch. You know that something so complicated and intricate could not have been made by chance. No amount of lapping of waves on shore could have resulted in anything like it. So you conclude that it was made by someone, deliberately, with skill and care. Now consider the Universe. It is much more complicated than a watch, so even less likely to have been created by chance. So there must be an equivalent of the watchmaker – a divine creator, God. So argued William Paley, very badly indeed. First of all, we know what sort of things watches are, and where they come from, so of course a watch points to a watchmaker. But, as David Hume pointed out, we have no idea what sorts of things create Universes. Experience is silent on that. What's worse, we know all sorts of things in nature grow and are not built: chickens come from eggs, not workshops. But, most fatally, Darwin's theory of evolution does explain how complex life evolved, without a divine engineer. So, however plausible Paley seems, calling time on his watchmaker is well overdue.

**3-SECOND
BIOGRAPHIES**
WILLIAM PALEY
1743–1805

DAVID HUME
1711–1776

30-SECOND TEXT
Julian Baggini

Surely something as complex as a watch could not occur spontaneously – or could it? Throw its clockwork parts together at random and eventually they will fall together in the correct order. But take your time – you are going to need a great deal of it.

FIG. I.

PASCAL'S WAGER

the 30-second philosophy

Before he became a devout

Christian, the 17th-century mathematician Blaise Pascal was a gambler. He was the founder of probability theory and worked out a way of determining the monetary value of a gamble based on probabilities. Pascal claimed that deciding whether to believe in God is like a gamble. It is a bet on the proposition that God exists. If God exists, then the consequence of believing in him is eternal bliss, while hell awaits atheists and agnostics. On the other hand, if God doesn't exist, then the consequence of believing in him is, at worst, living a religiously correct life, while the consequence of not believing in him is continuing one's life as it is. Pascal observed that the consequences of not believing in God if He does exist are so awful, and the consequences, of believing in Him if he does exist so good that, even if one thought that the probability of God existing was very small, it would still be better to bet that He does exist.

3-SECOND THRASH
Pascal claimed he proved that the gamble of believing in God is worth a hell of a lot more than the gamble of remaining an agnostic or an atheist.

3-MINUTE THOUGHT
A difficulty with Pascal's argument is that it isn't so easy simply to decide what to believe and, in particular, to believe in God if one actually thinks that it is very unlikely that God exists. And, even if one could do that, it is not obvious that God (at least, the Christian God) would be inclined to reward a person who came to believe in him on the basis of placing a bet.

RELATED PHILOSOPHIES
see also
HUME AGAINST MIRACLES
page 112

3-SECOND BIOGRAPHY
BLAISE PASCAL
1623–1662

30-SECOND TEXT
Barry Loewer

God doesn't play dice, and He probably wouldn't be impressed if you gambled on whether to believe in Him or not.

HUME AGAINST MIRACLES

the 30-second philosophy

You're hearing reports that someone has been levitating in Basingstoke, England. If true, it would be a miracle: someone or something would have suspended or changed the laws of nature. Would it ever be rational for you to believe such reports? According to David Hume, it would not. His argument was essentially one of balancing probabilities. Has there ever been a genuine, confirmed instance of a true miracle? No. Have people often lied or been mistaken when they claim to have seen a miracle? Yes. So what is more likely in this case: yet another con or error, or that this time, a true miracle has actually occurred? Clearly it's more likely to be another false alarm. This is the case, even if you can't explain how the 'miracle' really worked. It is still more likely that there is some natural cause, which we may or may not discover eventually, than it is that the laws of nature have actually been suspended. The conclusion is, therefore, that there are never good, rational grounds to think a miracle has occurred. Faith might lead you to believe in miracles, but reason can never follow suit.

3-SECOND THRASH
It's always more believable that reports of miracles are unbelievable.

3-MINUTE THOUGHT
Is it true that a miracle requires breaking the laws of nature? Couldn't God, for example, arrange things so that the Red Sea parts to allow the Israelites to flee by natural means, but at exactly the right moment? Perhaps, but in order to fix the timing, at some stage the natural progression of cause and effect would have to be tampered with, and that would still mean interfering with the laws of nature.

RELATED PHILOSOPHIES
see also
PASCAL'S WAGER
page 110

3-SECOND BIOGRAPHY
DAVID HUME
1711–1776

30-SECOND TEXT
Julian Baggini

You might believe in miracles, but according to David Hume there is no reason to.

GRAND MOMENTS

a posteriori A Latin term which means 'from what is after'. Philosophers use it to refer to knowledge that comes after perceptual experience or depends upon experience for its justification.

a priori A Latin term which means 'from what is before'. Philosophers use it to refer to knowledge that comes before experience (so-called innate knowledge) or, less controversially, knowledge that does not depend on experience for its justification.

atom Derived from the Ancient Greek word *atomos*, meaning 'not cuttable'. The Atomists held that everything in the Universe was made up of tiny, indivisible building blocks, moving about in the void, and colliding and combining to form visible objects.

Epicurean Having to do with the philosophy of Epicurus, an ancient Greek Atomist, Hedonist and perhaps the earliest Empiricist. Sometimes the word points only to a misunderstanding of Epicurus' hedonistic, moral theory, and means, roughly, 'a person devoted to base, bodily pleasures'.

external world The world of objects as they exist apart from our experience of them, as opposed to our inner world of thoughts, perceptions, feelings and the like.

Forms Perfect, unchanging, paradigmatic concept-objects, or archetypes, of the many types of things we see all around us, as posited by Plato. There are, for example, many beautiful things – beautiful paintings, people, landscapes, musical scores, etc – and what they all have in common is that they resemble the Form, Beautiful. Contemplating the Beautiful, getting to know it, makes one a better judge of beautiful things. The Forms enabled Plato to find a bit of permanence out there, which he thought was necessary for the existence of genuine knowledge.

Good Possibly the ultimate Form, according to Plato. According to many commentators, Plato thought that one could only have wisdom – one could really know the other Forms – only after one grasped the Form of the Good.

ideas A component notion of George Berkeley's idealism. Ideas are the passive objects of human knowledge, which can exist only in the mind that perceives them.

indirect awareness Our precarious perceptual connection to the world. If we are directly aware of inner, mental representations of objects in the external world, then we are only indirectly aware of the external world.

material substratum A something, we know not what, supposedly underpinning our perceptions of physical objects. It's nothing but a philosopher's fiction, according to George Berkeley.

mind A component notion of George Berkeley's idealism. The mind is a container of ideas or, rather, a thing that knows them, and acts upon them.

purpose A fundamental feature of almost any explanation, for Aristotle. While modern science attempts to understand things by viewing them as purposeless, Aristotle saw purposes, goals and ends everywhere: smoke rises because it 'aims for the heavens', acorns grow because their end is an oak tree, and so on.

Sun The representation of the Form of the Good in Plato's cave allegory. Once outside the cave, one is able to see real objects, not just shadows. Just as we are able to see the objects in the world because of the light of the Sun, so, too, Plato suggests, can we understand the Forms once we apprehend the Good itself.

SOCRATES' METHOD

the 30-second philosophy

Socrates was said to be the

wisest man in Athens because he knew that he knew nothing. In the dialogues of Plato, Socrates attempted to spread such wisdom by going around asking people what they thought about a subject, and then asking them tricky questions until they contradicted themselves. For instance, in the dialogue *Republic,* he asks what 'justice' is, and Cephalus suggests it is telling the truth and paying your debts. So, Socrates asks, if you borrow a sword from someone, you owe it to them to give it back, right? But then, what if you know that the person who wants their sword back has gone raving mad? 'There have to be exceptions', admits Cephalus. So, then, in this case justice requires not giving someone what they are due. Cephalus has undermined his own argument, revealing he doesn't know what he thought he knew about justice. Socrates rests his case, and then starts on someone else. This method can seem very negative, but if you want to end up with true beliefs, you have to test the ones you have very thoroughly, and Socrates' contention was that, if you do so, you'll find that most of what you think is wrong.

3-SECOND THRASH
Ask questions, pick holes, and convince people they don't know what they're talking about.

3-MINUTE THOUGHT
Many have adopted what they call a 'Socratic method', although this often bears little resemblance to the highly negative approach of Socrates himself. Sometimes, the term is broadly used to refer to a rigorous examination of ideas by means of question and answer. Others in the practical philosophy movement have developed Socratic dialogue, in which the discussion is very democratic and co-operative – utterly unlike the way in which Socrates destroyed the arguments of his interlocutors.

RELATED PHILOSOPHIES
see also
HEGEL'S DIALECTIC
page 132

3-SECOND BIOGRAPHIES
SOCRATES
469–399 BC

PLATO
428/27–348/47 BC

30-SECOND TEXT
Julian Baggini

Socrates was wise;
Socrates was a man;
all men are wise.
No, hang on, that
can't be right.
Let's try it again.

PLATO'S CAVE

the 30-second philosophy

RELATED PHILOSOPHIES
see also
BERKELEY'S IDEALISM
page 128

MOORE'S COMMON SENSE
page 136

3-SECOND BIOGRAPHIES
PLATO
428/27–348/47 BC

SOCRATES
469–399 BC

30-SECOND TEXT
Julian Baggini

3-SECOND THRASH
We're brain-dead believers in illusions, more likely to be blinded by the light than actually to see it – apart from philosophers, of course.

3-MINUTE THOUGHT
Don't be comforted by the thought that today's cave-dwellers are only those who sit transfixed by the television. Plato's cave is harder to escape than that. Not only artists, but also physical scientists are, in Plato's view, not attending to the most fundamental things. This invites the question, if Plato's truth lies outside of the physical world, does it even exist? Is it possible, or even desirable, to leave the cave at all?

Here is a picture of the human condition. People sit in a dark cave, watching shadows cast on the wall, thinking that they are seeing reality. If you were to take one of these people into the light of day, they would be so dazzled that they could not see. But, given time, they could look around, see the real world, and even the source of all that illuminates it: the Sun. Were they to go back into the cave, however, and try and explain the truth to the cave-dwellers, they would not only be laughed at, they would be killed. This is Plato's cave, one of the most vivid and memorable metaphors of all time. It is not that difficult to decode. The cave-dwellers are the ignorant masses; the shadows are particular, physical, transient objects, rather than the eternal, universal 'forms' of which all worldly things are pale imitations; the person who escapes the cave is the philosopher; the Sun is The Good, the source of all truth; and the death at the end alludes to the execution of Socrates, whom Plato describes as presenting the allegory, prefiguring his own demise. The moral? The rewards of philosophy are not acclaim, fame and riches.

If you live in a cave, think twice before going outside. You'll never be able to go back home again.

ARISTOTLE'S FOUR CAUSES

the 30-second philosophy

There is no doubt that the ancient Greek philosopher Aristotle was a rare genius. Not only did he bring rigour and clarity to every discipline he touched, but he also invented whole new disciplines. One of the intellectual tools he uses in this endeavour is called 'the four causes'. For any 'why' question you might ask about a thing, he argues, there are four sorts of answer, four explanatory causes of that thing, which can be identified. To borrow Aristotle's example, we can answer the question, 'Why is that a statue?' in four different ways. We can say (1) it's a statue because it is made of the stuff statues are made of, maybe bronze or stone (its material cause); we can say (2) it's a statue because that is the kind of thing it is (its formal cause); we can say (3) it's a statue because it was made by a sculptor (its efficient cause); and finally, we can say (4) it is a statue because it is doing what statues are supposed to do – maybe it is decorating a room (its final cause). To know the four causes is to know not only the physical facts of a thing, but also to understand its point and purpose.

RELATED PHILOSOPHIES
see also
RUSSELL'S THEORY OF DESCRIPTIONS
page 22

3-SECOND BIOGRAPHY
ARISTOTLE
384–322 BC

30-SECOND TEXT
James Garvey

3-SECOND THRASH
Why, you ask?

3-MINUTE THOUGHT
It's not only statues but also natural objects that have points and purposes, according to Aristotle. The purpose of an acorn, for example, is to become an oak tree. If you don't know that, you don't really understand an acorn, or so Aristotle thought. It took a lot – 2,000 years of thinking and another rare genius, Charles Darwin (1809–1882) – to take us beyond seeing Aristotelian purposes everywhere.

Aristotle liked to give very complete answers – every question had at least four.

LUCRETIUS' ATOMISM

the 30-second philosophy

Even if Lucretius' poem, 'The Nature of Things', said nothing much of philosophical interest, we would still read it for its exceptional beauty. But his work is also antiquity's most illuminating expression of the Epicurean world-view, and this makes it philosophically extraordinary, too. Epicurus (341–270 BC) held that everything was composed of tiny, indestructible atoms, jostling about in empty space. Lucretius carries atomism further still, though he pays homage to Epicurus on nearly every page of his poem. He fleshes out a thoroughly naturalistic conception of things, a view of the Universe as utterly purposeless and mechanistic. There is more than cold comfort in the purposelessness, however. Human beings are no longer subject to the whims of the gods, nor are we caught in the crosshairs of Fate. For Lucretius, supernatural explanations of events seemed not just odd, but ridiculous, even childish. In his hands, atomism becomes something like a full-blooded, philosophical position, not merely a proposition. From the atomists' vantage point, atoms in the void combine this way and that to form absolutely everything. They are all we need to understand not just our world, but ourselves as well. Lucretius' views constitute a large departure from religious superstition. In his poetry, the human race grows up a little.

RELATED PHILOSOPHIES
see also
LAPLACE'S DEMON, DETERMINISM, & FREE WILL
page 74

3-SECOND BIOGRAPHIES
LUCRETIUS
99–55 BC

ROBERT BOYLE
1627–1691 BC

30-SECOND TEXT
James Garvey

Sixteen centuries before the first chemists, Lucretius replaced earth, wind, fire and water with a world made of tiny atoms.

1889
Born, Vienna, Austria-Hungary

1911
Arrives at Cambridge to study philosophy with Bertrand Russell

1922
Tractatus Logico-Philosophicus published

1927
Starts discussions with some members of the Vienna Circle

1929
Returns to Cambridge, taking up a lecturing position there a year later

1939
Appointed to a chair at Cambridge

1947
Resigns from Cambridge

1951
Dies, in Cambridge

1953
His second great work, *Philosophical Investigations*, is published

LUDWIG WITTGENSTEIN

Ludwig Wittgenstein is

considered by many people to be the 20th century's most important philosopher. It is somewhat ironic, then, that perhaps what is best known about his life is that he waved a poker at fellow philosopher Karl Popper (1902–1994) during a dispute over moral rules at the Cambridge Moral Science Club in October 1946. This event is testament to a life that was lived with a compelling, though sometimes tragic, intensity.

Wittgenstein was born in Vienna on April 26, 1889, into the family of an affluent Austrian industrialist. His formal education was unorthodox (indeed, he didn't attend school at all until he was 14), but he nevertheless managed to secure a place at Manchester University to read engineering. It was here that he became interested in philosophy, and on the advice of the philosopher Gottlob Frege (1848–1925), he went to Cambridge in 1911 to study with Bertrand Russell (1872–1970).

He did not stay at Cambridge for long, but it was immediately clear that he had a brilliant mind. He wrote the manuscript that would become his first great work, *Tractatus Logico-Philosophicus*, while serving on the Eastern Front during World War One. However, after the book's publication in 1922, Wittgenstein gave up philosophy completely to become a schoolteacher and then a gardener. It took about five years for his interest in philosophy to be rekindled, when he began to talk with the Vienna Circle group of philosophers. He came to think that perhaps the approach he had taken in the *Tractatus* had been mistaken. This dawning realization led to the second phase of his career, during which he taught at Trinity College, Cambridge, and pioneered the approach that would become 'ordinary language philosophy' after World War Two.

Wittgenstein died in 1951 at the age of 62, but not before completing his second work of genius, the posthumously published *Philosophical Investigations*, in which he set out his new ideas about meaning and language.

BERKELEY'S IDEALISM

the 30-second philosophy

RELATED PHILOSOPHIES
see also
PLATO'S CAVE
page 120

WITTGENSTEIN'S PICTURE
THEORY OF LANGUAGE
page 138

3-SECOND BIOGRAPHY
GEORGE BERKELEY
1685–1753

30-SECOND TEXT
James Garvey

3-SECOND THRASH
According to Berkeley,
it's all in your head.

3-MINUTE THOUGHT
If this apple can only exist
in the mind that perceives
it, does it just wink out of
existence whenever I close
my eyes? Berkeley argues
that God perceives, and
therefore sustains, the
whole of the Universe,
whether we happen to
be looking at it or not.
Many take this answer to
be merely *ad hoc*, but for
Berkeley the continued
existence of everything is
proof not only of God's
existence, but also of His
benevolence.

Maybe we all accept that our senses provide us with a mental picture of the world, but not everyone understands what this implies. It means that we are only indirectly aware of the world via our inner, mental representations of it. If you are a sceptical sort, you might wonder how we know that our mental images really represent the stuff out there. George Berkeley's astonishing answer to this sceptical worry was idealism – denying the existence of everything, other than minds and the ideas within them. There is no room for scepticism about the external world, because there is no external world, no matter underpinning our experience. There are still things, in a sense. We group our regularly occurring, sensory experiences together and give them names. 'Apple' is our word for a consistent collection of sweet, red, crunchy sensations. That's all an apple is, for Berkeley. To suppose that it is something more, something out there, is to go beyond the evidence of experience. Worse, it is to think the absurd thought that sweetness can exist untasted, that red can exist unseen. If you disagree, bear in mind that you are the one claiming something more, some material substratum in addition to the evidence of our senses. The burden of proof, Berkeley might say, rests with you.

Without the means to perceive the Universe, would any of it exist?

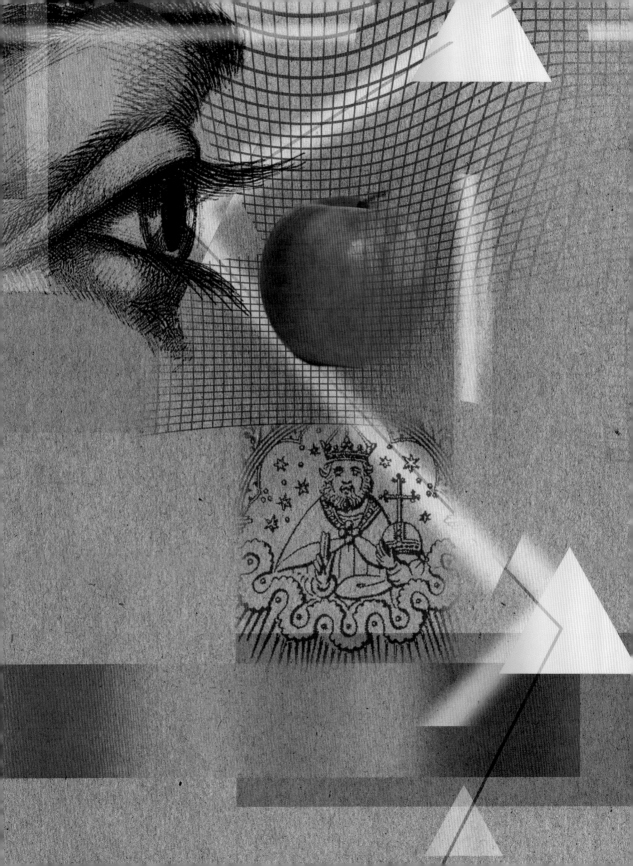

KANT'S SYNTHETIC *A PRIORI*

the 30-second philosophy

3-SECOND THRASH
True metaphysical claims do not just say weird things – they *are* weird things.

3-MINUTE THOUGHT
If Kant is right about metaphysical claims being odd hybrids, he's managed to explain why rationalists and empiricists have such trouble securing metaphysical truths. Rationalists seek truth through reflection, and empiricists justify beliefs via experience. If Kant is right, an entirely new approach to metaphysics is required. Kant's new approach, in the end, probably changed the entire course of Western philosophy.

Brace yourself for two difficult distinctions. Immanuel Kant distinguishes between analytic and synthetic propositions. A proposition is analytic if its predicates are contained within its subject. A proposition is synthetic if it adds new predicates to the subject. So, 'triangles are three-sided' is analytic (because 'three-sidedness' is in the concept 'triangle'). 'Triangles make excellent sails' is synthetic (because this fact about sails is not a part of the concept 'triangular'). Kant also distinguishes between *a priori* and *a posteriori* knowledge. *A priori* knowledge is secured by reflection, while *a posteriori* knowledge requires empirical research. So it looks as if analytic propositions can be arrived at by *a priori* reflection alone, and synthetic propositions require a bit of *a posteriori* digging. Here's the rub. Kant argues that metaphysical truths must be weird, synthetic, *a priori* hybrids: sentences both informative and known, without recourse to experience. They must be synthetic (and say something new that is not contained within the subject), yet *a priori* (and arrived at independently of experience). For example, 'Every event has a cause' smells like a synthetic, *a priori* statement. The concept of 'event' does not contain 'cause' within it, and there's no way our limited experiences could secure a general claim about every event throughout time having a cause.

RELATED PHILOSOPHIES
see also
FODOR'S LANGUAGE OF THOUGHT
page 60

3-SECOND BIOGRAPHY
IMMANUEL KANT
1724–1804

30-SECOND TEXT
James Garvey

Immanuel Kant figured out how a belief can also be true. Sounds strange? That's because it is.

HEGEL'S DIALECTIC

the 30-second philosophy

3-SECOND THRASH
History progresses by means of a dialectical process, which occurs as Absolute Spirit develops an increasingly sophisticated and accurate understanding of itself as being identical with the whole of reality.

3-MINUTE THOUGHT
The difficulty of Hegel's prose has led some to suspect that he deliberately obfuscated to create the appearance of profundity where none existed. The rise of logical positivism, with its claim that statements are meaningful only if they are true by definition or empirically verifiable, undermined the appeal of Hegel's philosophy. For many, Hegel's kind of philosophy is precisely what has to be avoided in order to produce good work.

G. W. F. Hegel believed that the aim of philosophy is to develop the conceptual apparatus necessary to understand the whole of reality, or, as he called it, 'Absolute Spirit'. Progress towards this goal occurs via a dialectical process, whereby less adequate conceptions of reality are overcome by, but nevertheless retained within, the improved conceptions that replace them. The dialectic has a triadic structure: in general terms, the idea is that any given concept or phenomenon (thesis) will manifest within itself contradictory aspects (antithesis), which require a movement towards resolution (synthesis). Thus, a particular concept or thesis (Concept 1) will not be sufficient to describe reality, and will contain within itself contradictions that imply its opposite or antithesis (Concept 2). The solution to this tension is a movement towards a synthesis (Concept 3), which preserves the original thesis and antithesis, while negating their logical opposition. This is an ongoing process. Concept 3 will become a new thesis, which will contain within itself its own antithesis (Concept 4), thus compelling movement towards a further synthesis (Concept 5). According to Hegel, dialectical progress will continue in this manner until the Absolute Spirit becomes aware of itself as pure freedom.

RELATED PHILOSOPHIES
see also
SOCRATES' METHOD
page 118

3-SECOND BIOGRAPHY
G. W. F. HEGEL
1770–1831

30-SECOND TEXT
Jeremy Stangroom

According to Hegel, our understanding of the Universe develops in a never-ending struggle between contradictions. As each opposing viewpoint is reasoned away, we edge ever closer to the truth.

JAMES' PRAGMATISM

the 30-second philosophy

Not many philosophical positions follow from reflection on squirrels, but William James' conception of pragmatism does. He says he returned from a walk in the woods to find his friends arguing about a man who tries to catch a glimpse of a squirrel that is moving in synch with him around a tree trunk. The man goes around the tree, and the squirrel is on the tree, but the question at issue was, does the man go around the squirrel? James' answer was to ask, well, what practical difference does it make to anyone if this or that answer is given? If it makes no difference, then the alternatives are practically the same, and the dispute is idle. If you swap reflection on squirrels for philosophical questions (e.g. Are we determined or free? Made of matter or mind?), you are on to a pithy, philosophical position, and you have a way of coming to conclusions in otherwise interminable, metaphysical disputes. There is a theory of truth in here, too. A belief is true if it helps us to get on with the practical business of living – if it's useful, helpful, and thus practical. For James, there is nothing more to the nature of truth than this.

RELATED PHILOSOPHIES
see also
MOORE'S COMMON SENSE
page 136

3-SECOND BIOGRAPHY
WILLIAM JAMES
1842–1910

30-SECOND TEXT
James Garvey

3-SECOND THRASH
The only differences that matter are practical differences.

3-MINUTE THOUGHT
Many object, probably rightly, to the implications of pragmatism for religion. James argues that in certain religious circumstances there's room for us to choose to believe what we find life-enhancing, helpful and useful. Maybe my belief that Jesus loves me gets me through the day, but is that enough for me to conclude that it's true?

Squirrelling around verbose, philosophical arguments is just a waste of time. According to James, if the arguments serve no purpose, they can never be really true.

MOORE'S COMMON SENSE

the 30-second philosophy

G. E. Moore took the

extraordinary step, philosophically speaking, of arguing for what everyone probably believes to be true anyway, what he calls 'the common-sense view of the world'. His view is a departure from a long philosophical tradition, going back to the Pre-Socratics, which holds that philosophy somehow reveals the true or underlying nature of the world by rejecting the ordinary beliefs we have about the way things are. According to Moore, our everyday, commonsensical beliefs are more or less right: there's an Earth which has been around for a while, and other people, and lots of objects, and I know all of this, and other people know all of this, too. He famously offers a 'proof' of the existence of external objects. He does this by holding up a hand and saying, as he makes a certain gesture, 'Here's a hand', and holding up his other hand and saying, with an accompanying gesture, 'Here's another'. Therefore the external world exists. It's a perfectly good proof, he argues, because the premises entail the conclusion and, further, the premises are different from the conclusion. Nothing is better known, he thought, than commonsense truths such as the existence of the external world.

RELATED PHILOSOPHIES
see also
JAMES' PRAGMATISM
page 134

3-SECOND BIOGRAPHY
G. E. MOORE
1873–1958

30-SECOND TEXT
James Garvey

3-SECOND THRASH
According to Moore, common sense beats scepticism hands down.

3-MINUTE THOUGHT
Maybe something deceptively deep is going on in Moore's defence of common sense. He's not merely marshalling premises in support of a conclusion. Perhaps he's pointing to a distinction between philosophically proving that a statement is true, and having grounds for commonsense knowledge. He knows he has hands (look, here they are), but maybe the sceptics are right, and he can't provide an argument for it. So what? It's our commonsense knowledge that matters most.

By simply using his common sense, Moore had the whole world in his hands.

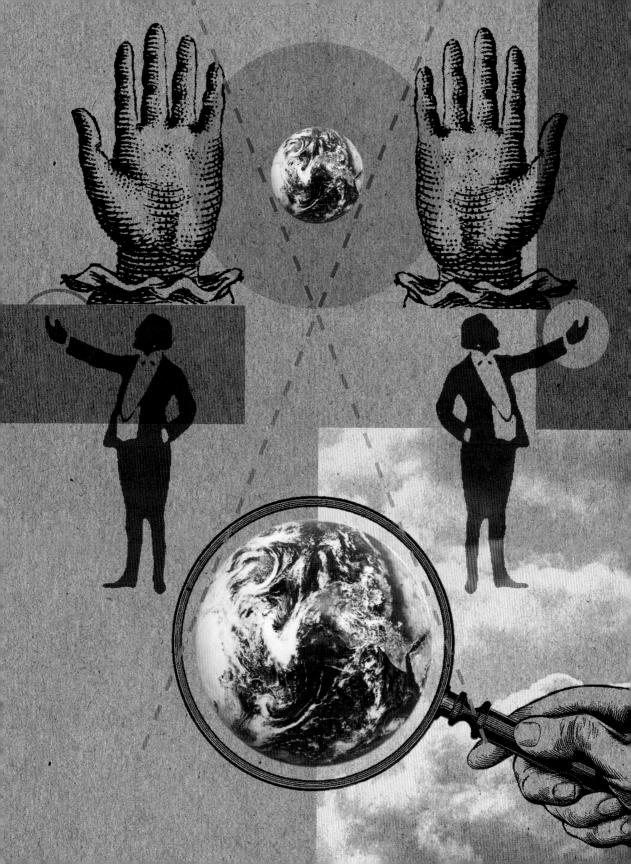

WITTGENSTEIN'S PICTURE THEORY OF LANGUAGE

the 30-second philosophy

3-SECOND THRASH
Wittgenstein's picture theory of language likens a sentence to an abstract picture, the structure of which pictures a possible situation.

3-MINUTE THOUGHT
Wittgenstein was a charismatic person. Although it was contrary to his intention, some of his followers treated him as a kind of cult figure, and even imitated his speech and gestures. Wittgenstein said that he became a philosopher because he was tormented by philosophical questions, but advised his followers against becoming philosophers.

Ludwig Wittgenstein was tormented by the questions of meaning and logic. In his *Tractatus Logico-Philosophicus*, he developed a 'picture theory' of meaning. The *Tractatus* begins with the proposition, 'The facts are everything that is the case', and ends with the proposition, 'Whereof we cannot speak thereof we must remain silent'. In between, in oracular fashion, Wittgenstein develops an account of language, logic and the world, in which the world consists of arrangements of simple objects into facts, and language succeeds in representing facts by picturing them. He likened language to modelling the positions of automobiles involved in an accident with the positions of toy cars. A simple, relational proposition 'Rab' pictures that the object 'a' bears a certain relation 'R' to the object 'b'. Wittgenstein thought that each meaningful sentence could be translated into an ideal, language sentence, composed of simple propositions, and the words 'or', 'and' and 'not'. Thus an ordinary sentence such as 'Dinner is on the table' is equivalent to a giant sentence composed of these words and simple propositions referring to basic objects. It is not clear exactly what simple propositions or simple objects are, yet Wittgenstein's work had an immense influence on 20th-century philosophy.

RELATED PHILOSOPHIES
see also
BERKELEY'S IDEALISM
page 128

3-SECOND BIOGRAPHY
LUDWIG WITTGENSTEIN
1889–1951

30-SECOND TEXT
Barry Loewer

For many, a picture speaks a thousand words. Wittgenstein's work suggests it is more like one word per image.

CONTINENTAL PHILOSOPHY

CONTINENTAL PHILOSOPHY
GLOSSARY

being The neglected subject matter of philosophy, according to Martin Heidegger. He has in mind not the particular beings studied by the sciences, but Being itself, 'that on the basis of which beings are already understood'. The only thing to do, he argues, is to undertake a complete reconsideration of the history of philosophy, tracing out our missteps in our misunderstanding of Being, from the ancient Greeks to the Modern era.

death of God Friedrich Nietzsche's shorthand for a crisis in value. Since we have intellectually negotiated the Enlightenment, he argues, we can no longer really believe in the otherworldly values offered by religious faith. God is dead to us, in the sense that we cannot genuinely buy into a value system predicated on religious superstitions. Something real is needed to ground a new value system.

deconstruction A branch of philosophy or critical method popularized by Jacques Derrida, whereby a text can be analyzed and found to have several meanings rather than a single, unified meaning.

dread A fundamental signpost on the way to understanding the nature of Nothing and, therefore, Being itself, according to Martin Heidegger. Dread arises when we contemplate our own mortality, the fact that our lives will end. It's a recognition of the nothingness that does more than await us – it shapes our very lives, makes our lives what they are. Heidegger sees this as a clue to the connection between Nothing and Being. For existentialist philosophers generally, dread has a connection to grasping the full implications of freedom, the thought that nothing is predetermined, and that one might do anything at all.

existentialism A collection of doctrines connected, at bottom, to the view that human beings create meaning in their lives by living, by choosing to exist in a certain way. The opposed and ancient view has it that meaning is fixed by the gods or, perhaps, that meaning is settled by something like an essential nature. Failure to recognize one's freedom is to live in bad faith.

hermeneutics The study of the interpretation of texts. An effort to find a way to understand the way someone else understands something.

nihilism A family of views that denies that objective meaning or genuine value attaches to some aspect of the human world. If God does not exist, some argue, then there is no objective source of morality, in particular, or value in general. Without this, no action is preferable to any other. Human existence, itself, is therefore pointless.

radical freedom The defining characteristic of our humanity, according to some existentialists. We may be unable to control the world we find ourselves in, but we have an absolute, even nauseating capacity to choose our own actions and, in a sense, create ourselves anew in each choice.

text For some in the deconstruction business, 'text' is not just the written word, but anything which is 'open to interpretation' – spoken lectures, pictures, architecture, even perceptual experiences.

Übermensch A German term variously translated as 'Superman', or 'Overman', with 'über' meaning 'superior', and 'mensch' referring to the human race generally. According to Friedrich Nietzsche, with the death of God, human beings face a crisis in value. Only something more than human, the Superman, is able to create value, and thus steer clear of the horrors of nihilism.

NIETZSCHE'S SUPERMAN

the 30-second philosophy

The German philosopher

Friedrich Nietzsche rather famously reported that God is dead, and for this reason many take him to be a nihilist, a subscriber to the view that nothing matters. But nihilism is his starting point, not his conclusion. His aim is to rescue us from it, not lead us to it. By saying that God is dead, Nietzsche draws to our attention a crisis in value. We moderns, he argues, have found our way through the Enlightenment and can no longer buy into the old value system, predicated as it is on religious superstition. If we have no value system, then we really are doomed, lost in a nihilistic sea. What we need is something more than human, a creator of new values in the world, a genuinely free being, who chooses what matters, and lives as he wishes. This is the Superman. Before you conclude that the Superman is kind of cool, bear in mind that you would find him comprehensively terrifying. The Superman, Nietzsche tells us, is a warrior, a conqueror, a concentration of ego, who cares only for himself and his own agenda. You and I would be ground underfoot like the wretched worms we are.

RELATED PHILOSOPHIES
see also
HEIDEGGER'S NOTHING
page 150

3-SECOND BIOGRAPHY
FRIEDRICH NIETZSCHE
1844–1900

30-SECOND TEXT
James Garvey

3-SECOND THRASH
Look, up in the sky, it's a bird, it's a plane – no, it's the Übermensch.

3-MINUTE THOUGHT
Nietzsche gets a lot of heat for the Superman, and it's true that parts of his thinking were misappropriated by the Nazis, and further misunderstood by many of his more simple-minded followers. All of this would have nauseated Nietzsche. He had choice words for racists in general, and German nationalists in particular. Both kinds of fools, he thought, were all too human.

Modern life has done away with angels and superstitions, and Nietzsche fills the void with a bigger and better version of ourselves.

1844
Born at Röcken

1864
Enrols at the
University of Bonn

1868
Meets Richard Wagner
for the first time

1869
Becomes Professor
of Philosophy at the
University of Basel

1872
The Birth of Tragedy
published

1879
Resigns from the
University of Basel

1883–1885
Thus Spake Zarathustra
published

1886
Beyond Good and Evil
published

1887
*On the Genealogy of
Morality* published

1900
Dies in Weimar

FRIEDRICH NIETZSCHE

In January 1889, Friedrich Nietzsche, the great German philosopher, who had written such luminous works as *Thus Spake Zarathustra*, *Beyond Good and Evil* and *On the Genealogy of Morality*, watched as a coachman whipped his horse in the Piazzo Carlo Aberto in Turin. This was more than he could bear and he collapsed. Madness had come to him, and he never again wrote another sane word.

The tragedy of Nietzsche's insanity was not unpredictable. His life had been difficult from the outset. Born in October 1844 into a Lutheran family, Nietzsche's father died from a brain illness when the young Friedrich was just four years old. However, this did not prevent Nietzsche from excelling at school, and then university, and, rather extraordinarily, he took up the Chair in Philology at the University of Basel when he was only 24. However, he suffered constant, debilitating ill-health, and in 1879 ailments such as migraines, eyesight problems and vomiting forced him to quit the University.

He spent the next ten years of his life shuffling between the boarding houses of Germany, Italy and Switzerland, almost always alone, and constantly sick. However, this was a remarkably productive period. In his final active year alone, he was able to complete *The Case of Wagner*, *Twilight of the Idols*, *The Antichrist*, *Ecce Homo* and *Nietzsche Contra Wagner*.

Nietzsche did not live long enough to witness the extent of his influence. He spent the remaining years of his life in a Basel asylum, and in the care of his mother, and then his sister (who was partly responsible for the later links between Nietzsche's ideas and National Socialism). He died on August 25, 1900, and was buried in the family plot.

DERRIDA'S DECONSTRUCTION

the 30-second philosophy

RELATED PHILOSOPHIES
see also
FODOR'S LANGUAGE OF
THOUGHT
page 60

3-SECOND THRASH
A deconstructive reading
will penetrate beneath
the surface of a text,
thereby demonstrating
that whatever you thought
the text meant, it probably
meant the opposite.

3-MINUTE THOUGHT
In one sense, Derrida's
deconstructive method is
unobjectionable: people
have been looking at
texts to discover hidden
meanings for centuries.
However, there are
problems with Derrida's
approach. Not least, on
occasion, he seems to
suggest that the elusive
nature of language,
and the self-referential
character of a text, renders
moot the idea that words
refer to particular things in
the world. This threatens
the distinction between
truth and falsity

3-SECOND BIOGRAPHY
JACQUES DERRIDA
1930–2004

30-SECOND TEXT
Jeremy Stangroom

The idea that meaning is elusive,
contradictory, multilayered and indeterminate
runs through much of Jacques Derrida's work.
Simply put, deconstruction is a technique of
reading texts that puts their meaning radically
in doubt. It rejects the idea that there is a
single, correct interpretation of a text that is
determined by the standard meaning of its
words. Rather, one might read a text to tease
out its hidden contradictions or ambiguities; or
one might look at what a text doesn't say, in
the hope that what is absent might reveal more
about its meaning than what is present.

This approach throws into question the
primacy of authorial intent. Derrida did not
believe that intention was of no interest in
the process of deconstruction. Nevertheless,
there exists the possibility that a text might
mean something quite different from what
the author intended. In particular, its inner
logic might suggest a reading that is far
removed from how the text would normally be
interpreted. Deconstruction, then, is a method
that relies on subverting the surface appearance
of a text, in order to reveal hidden layers of
articulation. It attempts to show that texts
contain contradictory logics, which tend to be
overlooked in more orthodox treatments.

*Once deconstructed,
this text describes the
image to the right.
Or does it?*

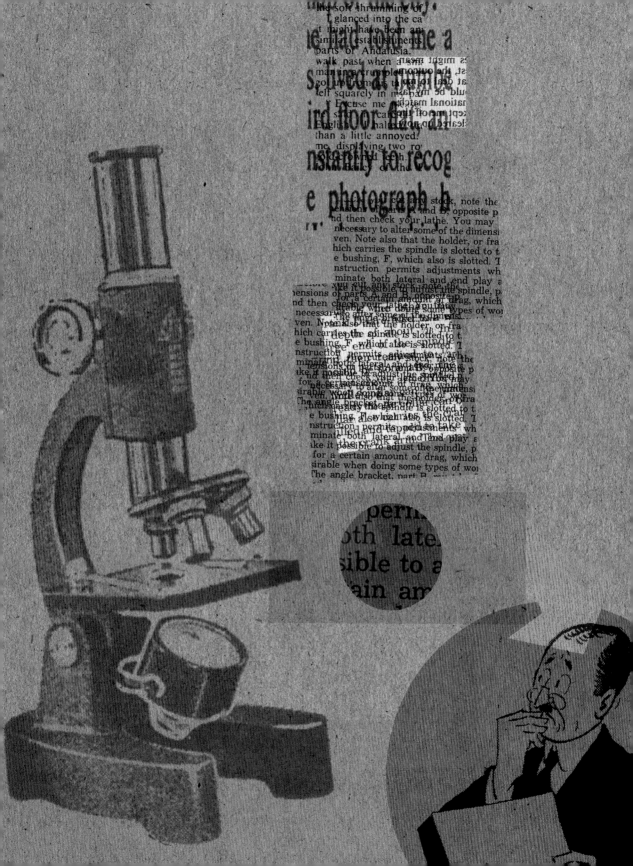

HEIDEGGER'S NOTHING

the 30-second philosophy

3-SECOND THRASH
Some say that Heidegger's views are much ado about nothing.

3-MINUTE THOUGHT
Stirring talk, maybe, but does it mean anything? Heidegger has been analytic philosophy's whipping boy since the middle of the last century, when those hoping to eliminate philosophical obscurantism took a critical interest in his writings. According to A. J. Ayer, Bertrand Russell and others, nothing is what you get when you try to pin down the meaning of Heidegger's writings.

The German philosopher Martin Heidegger argues that the history of Western philosophy rests on a mistake. Philosophers have always approached metaphysical questions in terms of this or that particular thing or being, but not Being itself; Being as such, whatever it is that enables individual things with properties to exist in the first place. A part of Heidegger's efforts to explore the nature of Being in this sense is a consideration of nothing. It leads to what might well be the first question of metaphysics, perhaps even the only true philosophical question: 'Why is there something rather than nothing?' In order to answer this question, we need to have some conception of nothing itself. Nothing is not any particular thing, or kind of thing, but it is not exactly an absence, either. In reflecting carefully on nothing, Heidegger argues, we experience dread, and this experience is our best clue to understanding the true nature of nothing. This feeling of dread has a lot to do with the inevitable nothingness that awaits us in death. In seeing nothing in this way, as our limit, or boundary, we can come to see nothing not as the opposite of Being, but as that which shapes and gives definition to Being as such.

RELATED PHILOSOPHIES
see also
I THINK THEREFORE I AM
page 36

NIETZSCHE'S SUPERMAN
page 144

3-SECOND BIOGRAPHIES
MARTIN HEIDEGGER
1889–1976

BERTRAND RUSSELL
1872–1970

A. J. AYER
1910–1989

30-SECOND TEXT
James Garvey

According to Martin Heidegger, underlying everything is nothingness – nada, nil, nothing at all. How does that make you feel?

SARTRE'S BAD FAITH

the 30-second philosophy

3-MINUTE THOUGHT
Sartre's conception of radical freedom is striking, but problematic. Timothy Sprigge has argued that it is insufficiently biological. Consider the example of a person intoxicated with alcohol. At least in part, their behaviour is a function of the effects of alcohol on their brain. However, if we allow that biology plays a role, why not also in the absence of alcohol? After all, behaviour is still a function of the brain, even if there are no intoxicating substances flowing through the bloodstream.

Jean-Paul Sartre, the French existentialist philosopher, famously argued that human beings are always and everywhere radically free. However, our freedom comes at a price: we experience anguish and uncertainty to the extent that we are aware that we are absolutely responsible for the choices that we make. The term 'bad faith' – *mauvaise foi* – refers to the strategies that we employ in order to deny the freedom that is inevitably ours. Normally this means taking on the guise of an inert object so that we can appear to ourselves as thing-like. In this way, we are able to deny that we are responsible for the choices that we make, thereby freeing us from the uncertainty of freedom. For example, confronted by a difficult moral decision, we might tell ourselves that we are compelled to act in a certain way because it is required by our job, or by conventional morality, or by the responsibility we have to our family. The reality, however, is that we can never escape our freedom, nor our awareness of it, since it is built into the very structure of consciousness. The paradox of bad faith is that we are simultaneously aware and not aware that we are free.

RELATED PHILOSOPHIES
see also
LAPLACE'S DEMON,
DETERMINISM & FREE WILL
page 74

3-SECOND BIOGRAPHIES
JEAN-PAUL SARTRE
1905–1980

TIMOTHY SPRIGGE
1932–2007

30-SECOND TEXT
Jeremy Stangroom

If we have another drink or a slice of cake, can we say that we were just following orders?

NOTES ON CONTRIBUTORS

EDITOR

Barry Loewer is Professor of Philosophy and Chair of the Philosophy department at Rutgers University, New Jersey. His interests include the metaphysical foundations of science, the philosophy of physics, and the philosophy of mind. He is co-author (with Georges Rey) of *Meaning in Mind* and (with Carl Gillett) of *Physicalism and its Discontents*. He has published many papers on the philosophy of quantum theory, the metaphysics of laws and chance, and the philosophy of mind.

FOREWORD

Stephen Law is the editor of the Royal Institute of Philosophy journal *THINK* – a source of philosophy aimed at the general public. He obtained his doctorate from Queen's College, Oxford University and currently lectures in philosophy at Heythrop College, University of London. He is the author of several publications, including *The Philosophy Files*, *The Philosophy Gym* and *The War For Children's Minds*.

WRITERS

Julian Baggini is the author of several books, including *The Pig that Wants to be Eaten and 99 Other Thought Experiments*, *Welcome to Everytown: A Journey in the English Mind* and *Complaint*. He is a co-founder and editor of *The Philosophers' Magazine*. He has written for many newspapers and magazines, including the *Guardian* and *The Herald*, and has regularly been a guest on many radio programs, including BBC Radio Four's *In Our Time*.

Kati Balog is a native of Hungary, but finished her philosophy degree in the United States, and is currently an Associate Professor of Philosophy at Yale University. Her primary areas of research are the philosophy of mind, and metaphysics. She is currently writing a monograph on the mind-body problem, and the nature of consciousness, but says she is also interested in what it is to be the same person over time, and what role our thinking about this issue plays in our psychology. She works in the analytic tradition, but also studies Buddhism, which has influenced her views in philosophy. In her spare time, she likes to hang out with her family, read, play the piano and travel.

James Garvey is Secretary of the Royal Institute of Philosophy. He has written several books, including *The Twenty Greatest Philosophy Books*, and was co-author of *The Great Philosophers*.

Jeremy Stangroom is co-founder and New Media editor of *The Philosophers' Magazine*. He is the author of numerous books, including *Why Truth Matters* (with Ophelia Benson), a *Prospect* magazine book of the year, and *What Scientists Think*. He has a PhD in social theory from the London School of Economics, and currently lives in Toronto, Canada.

RESOURCES

BOOKS

The Basic Writings of Nietzsche
Friedrich Nietzsche
Peter Gay (introduction)
Walter Kaufmann (translator)
(Modern Library, 2000)

Complete Works of Aristotle (Vols 1 & 2)
Aristotle J. Barnes (editor)
(Princeton University Press, 1971/1984)

The Collected Dialogues of Plato
Plato
Edith Hamilton, Huntington Cairns
(editors)
Lane Cooper (translator)
(Princeton University Press, 2005)

Conjectures and Refutations
Karl Popper
(Routledge, 2002)

The Conscious Mind
David J. Chalmers
(Oxford University Press, 1999)

Critique of Pure Reason
Immanuel Kant
Paul Guyer, Allen W. Wood (editors)
(Cambridge University Press, 1999)

Deconstruction for Beginners
Jim Powell
(For Beginners, 2008)

Gödel's Proof
Ernest Nagel and James R. Newman
(Taylor & Francis, 2007)

Fact, Fiction, and Forecast
Nelson Goodman
(Harvard University Press, 2006)

*Matter and Consciousness:
A Contemporary Introduction
to the Philosophy of Mind*
Paul M. Churchland
(MIT Press, 1988)

Meditations on First Philosophy
René Descartes
Michael Moriarty (translator)
(Oxford University Press, 2008)

A New Aristotle Reader
J.L. Ackrill (editor)
(Princeton University Press, 1988)

The Philosophy of Jean-Paul Sartre
Jean-Paul Sartre
(Vintage, 2003)

Think: A Compelling Introduction to Philosophy
Simon Blackburn
(Oxford Paperbacks, 2001)

A Treatise of Human Nature
David Hume
(Oxford University Press, 1967)

What Does It All Mean?
Thomas Nagel
(Oxford University Press, 1987)

Wittgenstein: A Very Short Introduction
A.C. Grayling
(Oxford University Press, 2001)

MAGAZINES/JOURNALS

The Philosophers' Magazine
www.philosophersnet.com

Philosophy NOW
www.philosophynow.org

THINK
www.royalinstitutephilosophy.org/page/34

WEBSITES

EpistemeLinks
www.epistemelinks.com/
Comprehensive list of links to philosophy resources on the Internet

Guide to Philosophy on the Internet
www.earlham.edu/~peters/philinks.htm
Classified list of philosophy resources

Philosophy Pages
www.philosophypages.com
Aids to the study of philosophy, including a study guide, dictionary, timeline, discussion of major philosophers and links to e-texts

INDEX

ACKNOWLEDGMENTS

PICTURE CREDITS
The publisher would like to thank the following
individuals and organizations for their kind
permission to reproduce the images in this book.
Every effort has been made to acknowledge the
pictures, however we apologize if there are any
unintentional omissions.

akg: 40, 88, 104, 126, 146
Corbis: 20; Bettmann: 64